Girl, You Deserve More

How to Break His Spell over You, Escape Your Toxic Partner, and Become Independent

CHRISTY PIPER

Copyright © 2021 by Christy Piper

Girl, You Deserve More: How to Break His Spell over You, Escape Your Toxic Partner, and Become Independent

All rights reserved. No part of this publication may be reproduced, distributed or transmitted in any form or by any means, including photocopying, recording, or other electronic or mechanical methods, without the prior written permission of the publisher, except in the case of brief quotations embodied in critical reviews and certain other noncommercial uses permitted by copyright law.

Although the author and publisher have made every effort to ensure that the information in this book was correct at press time, the author and publisher do not assume and hereby disclaim any liability to any party for any loss, damage, or disruption caused by errors or omissions, whether such errors or omissions result from negligence, accident, or any other cause.

Adherence to all applicable laws and regulations, including international, federal, state and local governing professional licensing, business practices, advertising, and all other aspects of doing business in the US, Canada or any other jurisdiction is the sole responsibility of the reader and consumer.

Neither the author nor the publisher assumes any responsibility or liability whatsoever on behalf of the consumer or reader of this material. Any perceived slight of any individual or organization is purely unintentional.

The resources in this book are provided for informational purposes only and should not be used to replace the specialized training and professional judgment of a health care or mental health care professional.

Neither the author nor the publisher can be held responsible for the use of the information provided within this book. Please always consult a trained professional before making any decision regarding treatment of yourself or others.

Library of Congress Control Number: 2021916111

ISBN: 978-1-956310-01-6 (hardcover), 978-1-956310-00-9 (paperback), 978-1-956310-02-3 (ebook), 978-1-956310-03-0 (audiobook)

Cover Design by Aaniyah Ahmed

Edited by Katie Chambers

Author website: www.christypiper.com

Special discounts are available on quantity purchases by nonprofits, associations, companies, book clubs, and more.

Bonus Content

Go to http://www.christypiper.com/gydm-bonus/ to claim your free *Freedom Checklist*.

Download your bonus Freedom Checklist

Note

I've used female and male pronouns in this book to reflect the most typical situation that I'm familiar with: a woman who is financially dependent on her toxic male partner and has trouble leaving him. While this situation could equally apply to same-gender partners, or where the male and female roles are reversed, the focus of my book is helping women leaving toxic male partners.

No liability is assumed for losses or damages due to the information provided. You are responsible for your own choices, actions, and results. You should consult your attorney for your specific questions and needs.

Some characters may represent a composite of people. Names and details have been changed to protect the guilty. My intention isn't to embarrass or expose them, even though they probably deserve it.

If you received this book as a gift, someone cares about you.

Contents

Introduction

If you picked up this book, you may be tired of your toxic partner and would've left a long time ago, but other factors stand in your way.

You may

• feel tied to him for financial reasons. Not wanting to lose your standard of living, you stay with him because you're afraid you won't get a job that pays enough to support yourself, or you don't feel confident enough to find any job.

• fear his anger and fear being kicked out if he finds out you plan to leave him.

• remember his good traits from the beginning, and still be in love with the version of him you thought he was.

• believe his promises that he will change for the better.

• consider him family and not want to lose that, especially if you don't have other family you can depend on.

• feel like you are too legally intertwined with him.

• feel like it's too late to leave and start over.

While these are all legitimate reasons to consider, when you are miserable, it's just not worth it.

You know you must leave, but you're not sure how. You know there are other people like you, who safely find a way out. But how did they do it?

Whatever reason holds you back, this book provides straightforward guidelines and considerations to smartly help you plan your escape. Girl, You Deserve More: *How to Break his Spell Over You, Leave Your Toxic Partner, and Become Independent* resolves your limiting beliefs and logistical concerns in a practical and easy-to-read manner. This book is for women who feel financially and mentally trapped in a relationship with someone they fear leaving.

I was one of these women. I've lived with two narcissistic partners and one toxic partner, who had a good heart but together we had a bad relationship dynamic. I left four different times, under different circumstances each time. Yes, you counted correctly. This means I left the same partner twice! So I understand the pitfalls of going back after escaping too.

Each time I realized it was time to leave, I either had low or no income. In three out of the four situations, I also had no family and few friends nearby. I was truly on my own. By the end, I was so mentally exhausted—but each time, I landed on my feet. If I could do it, you can do it too!

Ever since leaving these guys and starting my new life, I've become a go-to person for these situations. Friends, acquaintances, and strangers tell me their stories, asking for my advice. Through others' and my experiences, I've seen which methods and examples worked the most effectively and have included them in this book. I've also included some very real pitfalls and bad examples to beware of.

Women from all walks of life have already found great success by implementing these tried-and-true strategies and knowledge contained in this book. Knowledge truly is power!

Sarah, a woman who used methods in this book to leave her toxic partner, said, "The best thing about this book is that it addresses concerns that I was too embarrassed to ask about or didn't even know to ask about. It made me feel confident that leaving was actually doable."

Who this book is for

A woman who has a toxic partner but is stuck and has convinced herself she can't leave for various reasons, or she knows she should leave but isn't sure how to do it. She may feel financially dependent on her partner. She once loved him and thought they were soulmates. He said everything she wanted to hear and more. But after moving in together, everything changed. This book is for those women who may have tried to work it out with their partner, pleading for them to change. She may have suggested therapy or ways to compromise, but he refused and blamed her instead.

It is for the woman who has given up because her partner puts no effort into trying to change and doesn't care about her happiness. He may be a compulsive liar or cheater. He may lead a secret life he doesn't want her to know about. He may throw angry fits that scare her, and she doesn't know what mood he will be in when he comes home.

It's for the woman whose man makes her feel worse about herself instead of feeling supported. Her mental health is deteriorating, and she's not sure how much more she can take.

He doesn't need to be diagnosed

A toxic partner is someone whose behaviors leave you frequently emotionally, and sometimes physically, damaged. Often toxic partners have narcissistic personality disorder (NPD), borderline personality disorder (BPD), bipolar disorder, psychopathy, and sociopathy. These individuals are emotionally stunted, putting out negative energy onto those closest to them, making others feel constantly exhausted. They can anger easily and be dangerous.

However, these diagnoses are seldom given. It is very hard to diagnose someone who won't go in for help. And if they do go in, they can change their persona to charm the therapist. So you don't need an official diagnosis to know if a person is toxic to your mental well-being or not.

I originally wrote this book for those who want to leave a partner with NPD. But then I realized some people don't know what that is or their partner hasn't been diagnosed, so I did not want to limit the scope of who this book can help.

Besides, other types of toxic partners may not fall into one of these categories, but they can still be dangerous.

Who this book is not for

A married woman who has gotten into a few disagreements with her husband, but they have not been to marriage counseling and have not tried to sit down and resolve their issues. And overall, her husband is a good man and has kept his promises. Essentially, he did not "change" once they got married, but rather they are discovering marriage has challenges and compromise can be hard.

In this case, leaving the spouse doesn't fix the problems.

It also isn't for someone who lives with her boyfriend and wants to break up but doesn't fear leaving him. They just aren't compatible for the long run, and probably both realize it. Because he is a stable and reasonable person, he would be sad but will accept the breakup. In this case, all this secrecy is likely not necessary.

Who this book isn't for *yet*

A woman who isn't ready to leave her toxic partner. If she still hopes things will change and get better, she isn't ready to leave yet.

How to use this book

Treat this book as a reference manual. You can skip to the chapters most relevant to you and read that information first. If some chapters aren't relevant to your situation, skip them. Everyone's circumstances differ. Some people need more help figuring out different parts of the process.

The exercises and action steps in chapter 1 are designed to help you. You may frequently refer to your answers from chapter 1 to give you strength when you falter. They will remind you of your reasons for leaving, your future possibilities, and why you believe in yourself. But if the exercises slow you down too much, skip them for now. It's better to get through the chapters and benefit 80 percent than get stuck on an exercise and benefit 0 percent.

Figuring out your timeline

If your partner is dangerous or violent, you need to leave sooner rather than later. Some questions to help determine this:

• Has your partner ever physically hurt, grabbed, or blocked you?

• Have you ever seen him physically hurt anyone else?

• How quickly do you think you need to leave?

• Do you need to keep it a secret from him?

• Did he ask you to leave first? And if so, does he actually want you to leave?

The urgency to leave also hinges on your mental health.

If you need to get out immediately, you won't spend a lot of time thinking or talking about it. You will make a basic plan, choose a place to go, and go quickly. You might feel too drained or rushed to take the following precautions now. You may wait to take these steps until you move into a place where you feel safe.

It will also depend on how much money you have access to.

• Do you have a decent-paying job or a savings account?

• Can family members loan you money or a free place to stay for a while?

• Or will you need help looking into programs that offer financial help?

Do you already know where you will move to? Or will you need to weigh different options? This book will help you brainstorm creative ways to form an escape plan.

If you feel alone and can't talk to anyone about this, this book can help comfort you. If you don't have a great support system, this will also help give you ideas on what you can do for yourself.

Your strength is there; it is just dormant.

The longer you've been with him or the more legal ties you have, the harder it is to leave. Bad habits become harder to break over time. It's normal to become complacent and forget how easy it is to change your life. But since you are ready, I know you can do it!

What this book will do for you

I promise that you will feel more confident and prepared to leave if you follow the proven advice in this book. You will reclaim control over your life and gain your independence faster than if you needed to spend time trying to figure out all the logistics by yourself. Learn from the mistakes of others and what makes a success story. When you do so, you will feel safe and secure knowing you covered all your bases using this guide.

Don't be the person who stays with a partner who doesn't deserve you and then regrets it one day. You don't want to see life pass you by when you know you had the choice to leave and didn't.

Become the happy and confident you that other people will marvel at—a brave person who has broken the chains weighing them down and has conquered the mental barriers keeping them stuck.

One who finally started living life on her own terms. Start taking action today before any more of your precious time on this earth passes you by.

The following strategies on how to leave your toxic partner are proven to be empowering, effective, and life altering. To start learning these proven steps, all you have to do is keep reading. Each chapter will give you new insight into how you, too, can become a success story. Stop waiting around for something to change. You must be that change by taking control of your circumstances right now.

Commitment and Action

His hook: Your money and income situation

W ERE YOU IN A bad situation when you met your partner? Maybe you lost your job, a family member died, or you went through a bad breakup. You felt alone and had low confidence. Then when he showed up, he felt like the answer to all your prayers! This is how he hooks you in.

Mr. Nice Guy, your savior!

Not only was he nice to you but he also offered financial and material benefits. Maybe he gave you a free place to stay, let you use his credit card or car, gave you nice gifts, and put you on his health insurance plan. He acted like a caring family member, so you felt loyal to him in return.

Plus at first, he was super nice. Almost too nice. Knowing traits you admired in a person and traits women admire in general, he pretended to be that. He agreed with you on all the opinions you even hinted at. You felt like he shared all the same life values as you do.

Essentially, whatever your weak point or insecurity was, he found it.

He saw that these benefits were important to you and so gave them to you.

Jekyll and Hyde

Once you became dependent on him, he became less and less nice. Then when you moved in, things started *slowly* changing. It took a while to realize that something was very wrong. Your relationship gradually devolved into constant fighting, disrespect, and resentment. He stopped resembling the kind person you met a few months before.

This was done so slowly you didn't notice. If you slowly increase the heat = on a frog in water, he doesn't realize you are boiling him alive! If you do it too quickly, he will jump out. This is exactly what happened to you.

But you keep trying to bring him back, hoping the man you knew before would appear again. Where are your romantic words, breakfasts in bed, fun date nights, and all the positive attention and little goodies he showered on you before? Those do appear once in a while. And every time, you start to feel relieved again. You feel hopeful and happy and may forget about leaving.

And so you stay. Many of us stay with the wrong man for too long. Often because we start depending on him financially and emotionally. We love the higher standard of living, even though we dislike the way he treats us. For some, they never had a close family member they could depend on, and he fills that hole—sometimes. They don't want to lose that, so they don't leave. Is money or wanting to have a family keeping you hooked?

If you said yes, I'm glad you recognize this! *Because he does too.* That's the way he planned it. He knows his seemingly thoughtful little favors, financial stability, and his man-of-the-house image look attractive to women.

A toxic partner knows he's had trouble keeping women around in the past. He can't sustain the nice guy act for long, because his true personality *sucks*. So instead of you *wanting* to stay with him for his awesome, supportive, sweet personality, he uses money and/or your desire for a dependable family coupled with intermittent reinforcement to keep you hooked.

❧

Intermittent reinforcement—why you are emotionally addicted to him

He's measured out just how nice he needs to be and for how long, in order to keep you hooked. This is the phenomenon of intermittent feedback. He uses an unpredictable cycle of positive and negative reinforcement.

First, scientists ran continuous reinforcement studies on two groups of rats[1]. When the rats in Group A pushed the lever, a food pellet always came out. In Group B, no food pellets came out when the rats pushed the lever; these rats got bored and gave up. They behaved normally when the results were consistent and just went about their normal daily grooming patterns.

The rats in Group C received food pellets in unexpected intervals, also known as intermittent reinforcement. In other words, they never knew when pushing the lever would yield them a food pellet or not. Group C rats neglected their grooming, became anxious, and deteriorated over time. This inconsistency made the rats obsessed with pressing the lever, to the detriment of their own health.

This is an example of the power of intermittent reinforcement in both rats and humans. Abusers use this exact same method of unpredictable rewards to give you that dopamine high.

• Have you ever neglected your own needs while focusing on his erratic behavior?

• Have you ever lost sleep, gotten sick, or felt stressed due to worrying about what he'll do next?

• How many times have things permanently changed for the better?

This is a never-ending cycle. It will never get better. And the longer this goes on, the more it will undermine your self-esteem, and the worse you will feel. The deeper the rut you fall into, the harder it will be to dig yourself out. This can lead to feelings of craziness, depression, and even suicide.

If you're looking for validation from others who know him, you probably won't get it. Remember the first impression he made on you? He presented himself as a nice gentleman. Well, most of his friends and acquaintances still see him that way. If you try to find out if he's acted this way to others or complain about him, they won't know what you're talking about. Actually, they'll probably stick up for him, making you feel even worse.

If he is a narcissist or exhibits the traits, he's already said little negative things about you to others. He's positioned himself to look generous and caring while discrediting you so no one will believe you if you ever try to reveal the truth about him. This is one reason you feel so alone and crazy.

<u>Story time:</u>

When Jayne met Brad, she was sad about her parents' death. She wanted to take it slow, but Brad was very persistent. He bombarded her with sweet text messages and little gifts and quickly proclaimed his love for her. Additionally, he seemed to share all the same values on religion, politics, and family. He made a lot of promises and painted a beautiful picture of their future together.

Soon Jayne moved in with him. A year later, her life was nothing like she imagined. All the fun activities and surprises he used to do with her evaporated. He stopped being so generous. He even stopped having sex with her, claiming he lost interest.

Instead, he spent a lot more time at work or somewhere else, but not at home. Brad got pissed if she ever questioned his whereabouts. She caught him texting other women. He threw away and broke some of her belongings. Jayne spent many nights crying to her friends and planning to leave him. But as soon as he started acting nice for a few days, she would ditch her moving plans. He would always promise to change.

Jayne would get complacent again, saying she liked having a man around the house to fix things, she needed to stay on his health insurance, and various other reasons why it's better not to move. This happened so many times that her friends almost gave up on her.

But Brad's bad behavior continued to escalate, and Jayne had enough the day that Brad hit her and locked her out of the house. Her friends encouraged her to call the police. She did and was able to move out and get a restraining order.

≺≺≋

Your eyes are wide open

If you found the courage to pick up this book, you know there's a problem. You want to take action, but something is holding you back.

If someone never realizes something is wrong because it's all they've known, it's different. That person will be unhappy, but they won't know why and won't know how to solve their problem. They won't know any better.

That changes once you've seen the light.

> **Once you see something, you can't unsee it. You know exactly what's wrong and that you do deserve a better life. You know what you need to do to get there.**

The solution is often simple to say, but hard to do: leave him.

The average amount of times it takes for a woman to permanently leave her abuser is seven times, according to the Domestic Violence Hotline website [2]. It's not as simple as people think. So don't feel guilty. You're not alone. People who haven't been through this situation themselves don't understand why you are so attached and may think it is simple, but it's not.

The details may be more complicated due to other details, such as how long you've been together and if you're completely financially dependent on him. And most likely, you're still mentally and emotionally attached to him to some degree, even if you don't love him anymore.

There are a million excuses not to take action:

• convenience

• belief you can't do it on your own

• fear of loneliness

• fear you can't do better

• fear you'll lose your standard of living

• fear of his anger for leaving

• fear of others' judgment

• you are settled into a routine, know what to expect, and have a roof over your head

• fear being on your own could be worse because it's the unknown

• any other reason.

But your inaction and loss of freedom will haunt you forever now that you've seen the light. So if you have picked up this book, you recognize the issues and it is time to take action.

Exercise:

Spend five minutes writing down the biggest thing that's holding you back from leaving. It can be one big reason, or it can be five related, smaller ones. Include as many details as you need to paint a clear picture.

Then write down what your life will look like if you stay.

Then write down what your life will look like when you leave.

Put limiting beliefs to rest

To take action, you need to put limiting beliefs to rest. Right now, don't worry about whether you can sustain your lifestyle after you leave. Even if you currently live in a nice apartment in the middle of New York City or San Francisco, where rent is prohibitively expensive, just promise yourself to leave. And commit to finding a job and maintaining independence once you're out.

Worrying about not having enough when you leave and not earning enough income on your own is a limiting belief—one that he subtly embeds in your mind, directly or indirectly.

My ex used to tell me, "You'd never be able to survive without me." I'd survived great before I knew him for many years.

Another favorite was "You're so scattered. You just never get anything done. No wonder why you can't find a decent job." I'd had several good jobs, but when we moved, he convinced me to not work so I could stay home with our future kids.

Even worse was "You could never survive on your own. You need me to take care of you." I'd been working since age 16 and paid for all my own stuff until I met him.

Indirect attacks on your self-esteem also affect *how you see yourself* and lead you to feel *you must depend on him.*

> Also, the more successful you've been in an area, the more he will pick at you so you question your abilities. It is more of a challenge to undermine your biggest sources of pride and

competence.

Trust me, the more you hear it, the more it permeates your mind and you start to believe it. Abusers know the tricks of human nature.

One trick is that the more times something is repeated, people will believe it as fact—whether it's true or not is irrelevant.

<u>It happened to me, and it's happening to you too.</u>

Story time:

Your friends and family may be able to pick up on your negative, changing attitude before you do. I walked around the mall with my brother during semester break. I told him that I was thinking about dropping out of my PhD program. I said to him, "Maybe I'm just not cut out to be a researcher. It's boring anyway. I don't like the classes, and they're really hard. Maybe I'm meant to do something else."

My brother turned to me surprised, and said, "What?! Oh my God. Michael told you that, didn't he?" At first, I was confused, then he said, "Look, you never said anything like this before. You've been studying and taking prerequisites for years, just to get into this program. You've spent thousands of dollars and given up so much. Something has changed with you. Even if you think it's your idea, it wasn't."

I kept trying to justify it and reiterate the difficult math in the classes and how I wasn't liking it. "Of course, it's not fun; it's a PhD program! You knew what to expect! It's going to be hard!" He took a deep breath. "Have you seen the movie Inception? It's where Leo DiCaprio plants an idea in his wife's mind. *The idea spins out of control, and she eventually kills herself from it. But she thought the whole thing was her idea! But it was him all along. Trust me, watch it.*

"Also, remember when you won the departmental award and he didn't? I bet he's still jealous of you. Don't give up your career to move with him. If he can finish the program, you can too!" My brother looked at me in a self-assured way, as he chomped on some popcorn. At this time, my brother had more confidence in me than I did. He just didn't realize how deeply these beliefs were already ingrained in me. Neither did I.

Exercise

Think of the times he put you down. The times he told you that you won't get a job you want, or will never make as much money as him—statements that make it sound like you need him in order to survive or have a good life. This includes statements about being lucky to have him or ones that insult you in any way. Bad things he claims that others told him about you are likely not true either. Think of all these statements, whether you believe him or not.

Set a timer for 10 minutes and write down the negative words he has said to lower your self-esteem and lead you to believe you can't leave him. After you write down all the statements, come up with a counter-statement that goes against his statement, thinking of your true traits and skills that don't line up with what he said.

If you need help writing counter-statements, enlist the help of supportive friends or family. They can be your cheerleaders when you have trouble seeing it for yourself.

Examples of put-downs and counter-statements:

Example 1) Put-down: "You could never survive without me." The more independent you've been in the past, the more likely he is to say something like this because he's worried that you *can* survive without him. And he doesn't want you to try.

Counter-statement: Think about the times you've been independent and made money in the past. Write about your own history: "I've held a job since I was 16 years old, and bought two cars on my own. I've been out of the house and paying my own bills since I was 18. I've held good professional jobs. Even if those jobs aren't available right away, I can always go back to waiting tables if I need to make money. I paid my own bills before I met him."

Example 2) Put-down: "You'll never find a high-paying job in the city. No one will ever want to hire you." This is pure insult. If you're such a bad choice, why would he want you?

Counter-statement: Think about the past jobs you've had. "This may be a different city, but I've had good-paying professional jobs before. And I can find them again. I have the same college degree that he does. So it doesn't make sense that he thinks he deserves to make $100K plus, yet says I can't find a job like that. I am a likable, skilled, and dependable person, and always had more friends than him. Most companies here or anywhere else would be happy to hire me."

Example 3) Put-down: "Manhattan is so expensive. You'd never be able to afford your own place here. Good thing you have me." Your city may have a high cost of living, but he isn't telling the whole story. He's saying this to scare you.

Counter-statement: Think about alternative situations where you could still live in the area. "I can find decent places to rent a room for under $1,000 a month with roommates. I don't need my own one-bedroom, doorman apartment in the most expensive zip code. And if I ever wanted to get my own apartment just like this one, I'd just get higher-paying jobs until I could afford it."

Example 4) Put down: "If you didn't have me, you could go back and live with your parents. I don't want you to be homeless." He is giving you an illusion of false choices. This way you can picture how much your life will suck without him. And that you'd be forced to be a hobo or basement dweller.

Counter-statement: "Even if I got a part-time job making the lowest amount I've ever made—$12 per hour—I'd be able to afford to rent a bedroom in a four-bedroom apartment temporarily. Or I could ask my friend Stacey if I could rent a bedroom in her house temporarily. During this time, I'd find a professional job I'm more qualified for. Once I earn more money, I can move into the place of my choice. I would never have to go back and live with my parents or be homeless."

〜✎

Take action

Now that you have your limiting beliefs out of the way, you can start taking action. <u>But since leaving is a serious decision, knowing your level of commitment and your why will help you push forward.</u>

Some women get very fired up and ready to go when their partner does something bad to them. But as soon as he starts acting nice for a few minutes or days, she changes her mind and says she overreacted. Even though she spends more bad days than good with him, she constantly changes her mind, depending on his shifting moods. Consequently, she stays stuck in this cycle of misery for years.

When things get difficult, you'll need a reminder to keep moving, your why.

This exercise will help you determine your why.

Exercise:

For this exercise, you want to write down all the reasons you are leaving him. These can include:

• his unbearable personality traits

• the way he stops you from pursuing your own career

• the way you feel around him

• how the relationship affects your other relationships, etc.

You need to commit to this so you don't "forget" his bad behavior halfway through your plan. He will likely try to breadcrumb you and do something nice. Don't take the bait and decide to stay! This will only delay your plans and prolong your misery.

If you are mad right now, good. Use your emotions as fuel to write down everything *now*.

Step 1: Set a timer for 10 minutes. If you need longer or think of something later, you can always add to this list. Go!

Step 2: Go back to this list later and add a corresponding affirmative statement for what you want instead.

Examples

Example 1) Reason: "He causes fights and blames me for everything wrong in his life. He doesn't like the way I dress, doesn't like the way I clean the house, and blames me for not getting a promotion at work. He never says sorry. I always end up doing all the apologizing to calm things down. Even if it wasn't my fault."

Affirmative statement: "I want a partner who can work with me to solve issues and isn't afraid to say sorry or admit fault when warranted."

Example 2) Reason: "He promises one thing, but then does another. His actions don't line up with what he says at all. In fact, they are the opposite of what he says his beliefs and values are. Values he claims to have: Trust, honesty, compassion, and putting your partner above yourself."

Affirmative statement: "I want and deserve someone whose words line up with his actions. Someone who can keep promises."

Example 3) Reason: "When I disagree with something he says, he calls me stupid. Or sometimes gets in my face and yells at me. I'm afraid he might hurt me one day."

Affirmative statement: "I deserve someone who respects my opinions, even if we disagree. My partner should make me feel safe when we're together."

Example 4) Reason: "I want to use my college degree and become a professional [chef/ accountant/ teacher/ nurse/ economist]. But he doesn't want me to work. When moving, he only considers what city is best for his career."

Affirmative statement: "I deserve a partner who supports me in my endeavors and career choices. Someone who will consider me in joint decisions in what is best for both of our careers."

Example 5) Reason: "His family is mean to me or says bad things about me. He never sticks up for me. Sometimes he even takes their side."

Affirmative statement: "I deserve a partner who says good things about me and sticks up for me in front of others."

⊷≪⊷

When to take action

You definitely want to take action if your partner is irredeemable, right? If he can't or won't change, your relationship can't get better. This is especially true if you suspect he has a mental health disorder that he isn't getting help for, such as NPD, BPD, bipolar disorder, psychopathy, or sociopathy.

If he blames you for his life issues, he can't take responsibility for himself. He may blame you for

• arriving late to work

• staying up too late

• causing a fight that he provoked

• not being prepared for his meeting

• not cleaning the house well enough

• or speeding through a red light and getting a ticket

He may belittle you privately or in front of his friends.

If he complains to his family or friends about you instead of defending you, this won't get better. He sees you as a scapegoat, not a partner.

Has he ever hurt you physically, broken your belongings, chased you, or scared you? Is he an addict, compulsive liar, cheater, or owes unpaid debts to you or others? These are ingrained character flaws. He likely learned these patterns from childhood. These often formed as a survival mechanism, which he still relies on today.

The good news is, his insults and anger have nothing to do with you. The bad news is, it's extremely hard to change someone's programming—especially when they don't see it as a problem and won't put in the effort to change.

You don't deserve to be collateral damage.

What would he do if you started treating him the same way he treats you? Does he have double standards that don't apply to him? It's not fair if he thinks he deserves good treatment, but you don't deserve it.

Actions speak louder than words. Always watch his actions. Too many women take words too seriously. They believe his promises, but never actually hold him to it. I get it. You *want* to believe it. So you hold out hope.

But remember, your eyes are wide open. Deep down, you know things won't get better long term and he is not going to change. You don't believe his promises anymore. But if you picked up this book, you might find it hard to leave. Don't worry. I am going to help you.

Moving beyond talking to doing

You likely researched other information about your relationship before this book.

Maybe a concerned friend or family member gave you advice. You may have found a YouTube video about abusive behavior or read books about emotionally distant, wounded, or narcissistic men. Maybe you joined NPD abuse forums, or other types of abuse forums, on Facebook.

You might have learned that your partner is a narcissist, psychopath, borderline, bipolar, or just too damaged from previous relationships or from his own family. You watch video after video, taking in all this information.

This is great when you're trying to figure out a problem or confirm something. But at some point, you know enough. You know you need to take action.

> **You can spend months or even years researching. But you already know what the problem is and how to solve it.**

How much extra research do you need to do? What do you still need to figure out?

Yes, joining online forums is helpful. When you do this, you instantly connect with others who are going through the same thing. You see so many similarities between your situations. Many narcissistic abuse forums have huge memberships. It's a relief to know you aren't the only one.

Engaged members know a wealth of information, share similar personal frustrations, and listen to you rant about yours.

But this is a double-edged sword. On the one hand, these can be comforting if used correctly. It can be a place to empathize with others who've gone through the same thing. <u>It can serve as an excellent place to exchange information, stories, encouragement, motivation, and tips on how to best take action and leave.</u>

It's refreshing to connect with others going through the same trials and tribulations as you—especially since you probably can't talk about it in your everyday life to coworkers and neighbors. Even if you did, many of them wouldn't get it. Since these problems are internal and not external, it's hard for outsiders to fully comprehend.

However, on the other side of the sword, you may realize many people in these forums like to rant and aren't changing their situation.

It's easy for people to stay in complaint mode forever and not take any action. They get stuck feeling sorry for themselves and talking about their problems, passing their stressful energy onto others. But they don't ever actually leave. It's almost as if these people get addicted to their misery.

Many complain, feel better, then have just enough energy just to stay in their bad relationship. This behavior keeps you stuck in a holding pattern of inaction.

You need to change your mindset into fixing your life, instead of complaining about your life.

Others' energy and thought patterns become contagious the more time you spend around it. Have you heard the saying "You are the average of the five people you spend the most time with"? This includes people in online forums. Remember this when you spend time interacting in these forums.

You don't want to get stuck here with perpetual complainers who fail to change their lives—you need to start taking action.

Exercise:

Consider why you go to these forums. Is it for validation that you were right and he was in the wrong? To figure out what to do or say to him next? Do you feel like no one around you will believe or understand it? Is it to complain? Is it to learn how others got out of their situation?

Write down why you've spent time in these forums in the past and how much time you spend there.

Now if you plan to continue to visit these forums, write down what you plan on using the forum for. Include how much time you plan to spend there daily.

Set the timer for five minutes. *Go!*

Past: "I joined two narcissistic abuse forums to vent about my partner, and read others' stories. We all read and comment on each others' stories. We tell each other what jerks we picked out, and what rude things we say back to them. I spend more than two hours in there most days."

Future: "I will post a question in both forums: 'Has anyone left their toxic partner? How did you do it, and what are your best tips for preparing and doing it?' I will focus on the comments I get to these posts and stop venting and complaining. I want to take action. I'll spend 10–45 minutes each day reading the replies to help give me strength and inspiration to move forward."

Past: "I joined a paid relationship help forum. I chat with other women who have relationship problems and posted my story. Other members empathize with me and complain about their spouses and situation. The relationship expert moderators give tips on how to improve communication and become a better partner. I've tried their suggestions, but my husband doesn't respond positively. I spent one to three hours in the forum per day."

Future: "I want to cancel my membership soon since the tips aren't relevant to my situation. Most people there seem intent on staying in their relationships and can't seem to move on. They present the same problems month after month. I will ask a few questions to see if anyone gives advice on leaving. I will only seek advice on taking action to move out, and best practices. I will spend no more than 30 minutes per day in the forum. I will spend this newfound time to plan my move."

Why it's smart to collect evidence

Collecting evidence can be useful for several reasons, including needing a reminder to never go back! It can also give you that extra motivation boost when you feel like it's too hard. Anytime you have a weak moment, look at this reminder. This visual evidence will remind you why you can never go back to living this way.

You also may need legal evidence to back up your side of the story. *When in doubt, save evidence!*

These may include text messages or emails to other people, photos or social media posts of him with his other romantic interests, or his inappropriate comments to them. If he threatens or verbally abuses you, you can record his voice using your smartphone or a tiny digital voice recorder you keep in your pocket. You can find these tiny voice recorders for under $15 online. Be sure to check laws in your state, because in a few states, it's illegal to record without both parties' consent.

If he ever hurts you or the kids or pets, you can take pictures of any visual marks and bruises. Taking pictures of broken walls or furniture can help too. The doctor's office is a great place to report the truth of what happened. That way there's an official record of it with an expert's examination. If you feel shame or embarrassment about this—just remember that this evidence can free you of any claims he might make against you. And if kids are involved, this can help you get custody in court.

Evidence can also consist of bank account statements or receipts, showing any money he took out of your account or spent on strange things. An obvious example of this includes money he spent on other women if he's a cheater. This includes vacations, hotel rooms, or prostitutes.

That way if he tries to take you to court, smear your reputation, or sweet talk you to come back—you will always have proof about his true character.

You can also keep a written and dated log of these instances as supporting evidence. When he is used to being in control and then loses his partner, he may try to lash out any way he can. It's best to prepare yourself. See more information in the "gathering evidence" section in chapter 5.

Exercise:

Take pictures or screenshots of any damning evidence you've found—whether it's inappropriate text messages with other women, threatening text messages or emails to you, bills or receipts with shocking expenses, even his herpes diagnosis and prescription from cheating. Save these pictures in the cloud or email them to another email account, just in case something happens to your phone or camera. You don't want to lose these pictures!

In the meantime, please don't tell him that you are gathering this evidence! Also ensure that he can't ever find it in your email, phone, or elsewhere. I know it might be fun to taunt him, but it's not worth it. You don't want to tip him off that anything has changed. You also don't want him looking for and destroying your valuable evidence.

Believe in yourself and commit to leaving

For a while now, you have probably been complaining and obsessing about his behavior. Let's get you moving from that to committing to leaving. You are ready!

This book is about taking action. It's about taking back control of your life and moving forward. So buckle down, girlfriend. I know you can do this.

The simple fact that you're reading this book is an act of bravery.

Many women never even take that step. They see a glimpse of their potential future but then close that door. It's too scary for them to leave what they're used to. Yes, it is a scary world out there with many unknowns. I'm not going to pretend that it'll be easy at first. The physical actions themselves are easy—the mental hurdles aren't. It's going to feel worse before it feels better. But feel secure in the fact that things will eventually get better after you leave.

Exercise:

Write down your 10 best qualities or successes. They can be character traits, talents, accomplishments. Try to do this yourself. Don't be bashful. This list is for your eyes only. Ask your friends for their suggestions if you get stuck. If you think of more than 10 and can't decide, write them all down.

You can refer back to this list when you're feeling down or discouraged.

Set a timer for seven minutes. Go! You can always add more later.

Example list:

• People like me. My great smile wins people over and puts others in a better mood.

• I'm empathetic and caring, often lending an ear and shoulder to cry on when my friends are going through a hard time.

• I'm good with people and a hard worker. I won top salesperson at my company and made a huge bonus in addition to my sales commissions.

• I'm multitalented: I can play two instruments, drive a stick shift, and can play three sports.

- I'm smart. I graduated college with honors while holding down two jobs.

- I'm musically gifted and taught myself how to play guitar.

- I'm disciplined and smart. I taught myself how to speak another language.

- I'm hard working and my work ethic impresses people. I worked my way up from being a cashier to a manager position.

- I'm attractive and take good care of my body. I work out or do yoga at least three times a week.

- I have a good fashion sense. I frequently get compliments on my clothes and style.

- I'm helpful and people ask me for advice. My little brother loves me, looks up to me, and asks me for my advice.

- I'm resourceful. I can teach myself how to fix almost anything by watching YouTube videos.

Now use that belief in yourself to commit to leaving. Promise yourself right now that you are going to leave.

꙳

Chapter 1 review
His hook: Your money and income situation

- He found you at a vulnerable point in your life and felt like a Godsend.

• He gave you financial and emotional benefits that made you feel good.

• He did this on purpose: to make you dependent on him.

• He isn't who you thought he was and you know you should leave, but you don't want to lose your high standard of living and physical comfort.

• He knows his personality isn't enough to keep you around, so he bribes you with material comforts. He knows he's not nice to you.

Your eyes are wide open

• Because you know there's a problem, you can't ever un-know it.

• If you don't take action, what your life could have been will haunt you.

Put limiting beliefs to rest

• He shaped your limiting beliefs with his subtle comments and insults.

• The more times he says something, the more you subconsciously start to believe it. You may even believe you came up with the idea yourself.

When to take action

• Knowing your why will help you move forward when it gets hard.

• Because you picked up this book, you know something is wrong with your relationship. Your relationship is unredeemable, and you know you can't go on living like this. You're ready to take action.

• Forums can be supportive initially. You can learn more from others in a similar situation and exchange information, but don't get caught up in complaining without ever leaving.

• Many women get stuck in the complaining phase. They never shift their mindset to taking action to leave.

• "You are the average of the five people you spend the most time with." Remember this when you spend time in these forums.

• Recognize your bravery for reading this book and wanting change. Honor yourself by taking action. Your life can and will change for the better if you follow the steps laid out.

Why it's smart to collect evidence

• The photos serve as a great reminder anytime you think about going back.

• If he or anyone else questions your reality, you have the visual proof.

• Photographic evidence can serve as legal documentation in court.

• It can back up your case if he slanders you later.

Believe in yourself and commit to leaving

• You are ready to take action and leave.

• Remember your best traits and what you've accomplished in the past.

• If you can master those hard things, you have the power to leave and succeed on your own.

How did doing the exercises feel? Empowering? Does it help remind you of who you were before you met him and what you can do?

Now that you are feeling more confident and fired up about leaving, let's discuss the logistics of planning your move.

⁓❧

Original studies on rats and operant conditioning performed by B.F. Skinner; 1959.

National Domestic Violence Hotline website: www.thehotline.org.

CHAPTER 2

Logistics of Planning and Moving

Y OU CAN'T HALF-ASS YOUR effort to leave. You are either all in or not. Why? Because leaving an abusive relationship can be dangerous. According to the Domestic Violence Hotline, 75 percent of serious injuries happen when the survivor tries to end the relationship [1]. Depending on his predisposition to violence, this might apply to your situation. If he's never hit you before, there is always a first time for everything—especially when he knows he will lose you if he doesn't stop you.

> *And for women who return to their abuser, things don't get better. Coming back just proves how much control he holds over her.*

According to the Domestic Violence Hotline, a major reason women go back to their abuser is that they don't have a solid plan. This includes *not having:*

• enough money or resources

• a safe place to go

• a supportive person (friend, family member, social worker)

They also go back because they:

• hope and believe he will change

• fear his threats without question

• suffer from Stockholm syndrome (strong emotional bond to the abuser)

• don't have the necessary legal documents.

But since you are reading this book, you will have the advantage of a solid plan. So you won't run into these issues.

Please see more information in the "Protect your safety" section in chapter 4 about how to protect yourself once you move out.

Where to plan

It's best if you plan outside of your home. Don't take a chance that he'll find out about your plans. He knows more about your daily activities than you think.

If you must look something up while home, don't use your home internet connection. Use LTE data on your phone, but *only* if you are sure he isn't monitoring your phone. If he is good with computers or very paranoid, he could be monitoring the internet traffic and what websites you're visiting. He could also be monitoring your phone.

Definitely don't make phone calls at the house. He could be recording them, or he could come home early and overhear you.

So it's best to plan anywhere away from home and him. This could be at a coffee shop, library, friend's house, park bench, or school.

Your car isn't the best place because it could be bugged, so consider that before making phone calls in there.

What to be aware of as you plan

Your plan needs to account for all the ways he can keep tabs on you:

• Asking neighbors or friends about your whereabouts.

• Going through your phone records, text messages, or notes app.

• Looking over your shoulder to see you input your passwords.

• Reading your journal or planner.

• Checking credit card bills or receipts, especially if he has access to your mailed or online statements.

• Going through your purse.

• Placing a tracking device on your car.

• Installing spyware on your phone or computer.

• Planting recording devices (camera or audio) in the house or car.

• Going through your phone or computer's browser history or cookies.

Apple devices have a feature called "find my iPhone." It's good if you misplace your phone and want to find its location. But it also shows your location on any other synced Apple devices, such as a Mac computer or iPad. So if he has access to any of these connected devices, he'll know where you are at all times.

Someone who knows the password to one of your Apple devices could also see all your texts, phone calls, emails, and internet search history.

Also take note if your password to your device is the same as any other pin numbers he might know, such as the ATM.

Breaches into any of these could lead him to your escape plans and future home address.

Story time:

After Michael kicked me out on a whim and I'd been gone for a couple of weeks, he agreed to let a friend stop by to pick up a few things for me.

I told her to grab my iPad. He made a big deal about handing over my iPad. When I turned it on, I figured out why. The "find my iPhone" feature was switched on to track my iPhone location. Using my iPad, Michael could see everywhere I went! He later revealed that he read my texts and monitored my contacts and phone calls. While I'm not sure how he got my password, he must've seen me input my password. All it takes is one glance while you type it in.

Good thing my new building had good security, multiple floors, and was on a busy street! I believe these factors helped deter him from finding and cornering me.

To know if he has this kind of access to your phone, reflect back. Have you ever left your phone unattended? How about while you were in the shower, sleeping, or charging it? Is there a chance he could know your password?

If you are on a family plan with him, he has access to a lot of your info, even if he doesn't know your passwords and isn't tech savvy.

> *Being on his plan means he can walk into his phone carrier's store or login to his online account, request printouts of all the phone numbers you are sending texts to and calling, and see all the dates, times, and length of the phone calls.*

Even if the names aren't listed, he can do a quick online search to find out who you've been calling, especially if they are companies.

Planting spyware on your phone isn't as hard as you think. He only needs to access it once to monitor all your activity. He could also install software that monitors all internet traffic going through your home router.

Even if he doesn't install spyware, he could manually check your phone while you're not looking.

He could also use the old-school method of reviewing your phone statements.

It's best to play it safe and be extra vigilant now rather than sorry later.

Story time:

Once Shannon realized Dave was chatting with and meeting up with other women, she started going through his phone. It didn't matter that he had changed his password because she had seen him input his new password.

She waited until Dave fell asleep, then snuck into the living room with his phone and spent hours scrolling through his texts, Facebook, Skype, and WhatsApp messages.

When he took a shower, it gave her another opportunity to take a quick peek at his phone. It only took 5–10 minutes to keep her updated.

When Dave left the house, Shannon used his laptop. She skimmed all his internet history and emails, even the deleted ones in the trash can. She found out about events he was attending and even showed up to some of them. This is how she found out about Dave's secret life.

Your partner could be doing the same thing to you. He could find out every person you text, call, and email. And any websites you visit. Maybe you plan to erase your texts, call list, and browser history every day. But new ones come in, and you may forget to do it every time.

Story time:

My friend's stepdaughter, Michelle, has been married to Jonathan for over a decade. Jonathan insists that the entire family keep their phones downstairs in the kitchen to charge overnight. He talks about trust all the time. Because he proclaims it's an important value of his, Michelle assumed he was trustworthy as well.

But it turns out that he went through Michelle's and their daughters' phones. Emails sent to her personal account mysteriously got deleted, and Michelle claims she never saw them. But whenever her stepfather emailed her work account, she always received them.

Jonathan woke up every morning at 4 a.m. to get ready for work, while the rest of the family slept till 6 a.m. That gave him two hours every day to scroll through everyone's phones, especially his wife's.

Jonathan deleted emails from his wife's stepfather to keep her disconnected from extended family. She was in denial about this. Imagine what he would do if he found any evidence of Michelle planning to leave him?

～❦

Signs that he has likely been spying on you

There is no failsafe way to know if he has been accessing your phone or devices. But there are a few telltale signs that he could easily be monitoring you.

1. **He knows your password.** Either you've told him, he's seen you input it, it's the same password you always use, or you don't lock it with a password.

2. **You've seen him using your phone.** Maybe he uses it for legitimate reasons, such as mapping addresses you're going to together, paying bills, talking on it, or checking the weather. If he feels comfortable using it and already has it in his hands, it doesn't take much more effort to snoop.

3. **He's good with technology or has a phone like yours.** With this, he doesn't have a learning curve. He knows his way around your phone, so he can access and check its contents very quickly—all before you even notice it's been sitting in the other room next to him.

4. **He seems to know information you didn't tell him.** Sometimes you text a friend, research a topic, or write something in the notes app that you've never mentioned to him. Yet he seems to know about this already. He may even ask

you about it. This is almost a sure sign he has access to your phone or may have a recording device in the house.

5. **You have a shared computer or tablet.** He can easily see your browser history. This means if you visit a website, he'll find out about it. He can access any files you've downloaded.

> *If your shared computer or tablet is linked to your phone, he can access nearly all of your phone's information.*

This may include photos, contacts, email, websites visited, notes app, and files stored in the cloud. Be careful if you have any sensitive documents, such as bank information, credit card statements, or notes about moving.

6. **You have saved passwords or auto sign-in.** If you save your passwords, anyone who uses your computer can log in to any websites you have an account with. If it is set to auto sign-in, it's the same thing, except it's one less step because it's already logged in.

7. **You leave your computer screen on.** If you leave your computer on, it's an invitation for anyone to peek at what's on it. It's easy to password protect it and set the screen to automatically lock after a few minutes of no activity.

If you're wondering if this is overly paranoid thinking or that a normal person wouldn't do this, you are right. Toxic people are extremely paranoid and go to great lengths to keep their upper hand. So they employ spying techniques that most people would never think to do.

Story time:

Michael installed software on my laptop under the guise of being nice and helpful. Little did I know, he somehow extracted my email passwords and who knows what other private information. I didn't find out until many months later when we lived in separate cities.

He confronted me about a personal situation I didn't want him to know about. But I knew there was no way he could know about it, so I brushed it off. He kept digging in and mentioned names and details. He finally lost patience with me and started reading an old email I'd sent a friend.

This creeped me out. He'd probably been reading my emails for months! But I never would've found out if he hadn't confronted me about this incident.

How to avoid being spied on

If you visit the National Domestic Violence Hotline website, a "security alert" message immediately pops up warning that "internet usage can be monitored and is impossible to erase completely." This is a common problem that people with controlling partners face, which is why it's the first thing you see when you visit the website. Don't take this warning lightly.

To keep your planning safe from his spying, you can try one of these options. Please use discretion when considering these options.

1. Get a burner phone: This is your safest bet if you think he spies on you. You can find so many cheap phone options out now for your secondary phone.

You can even just buy reloadable minutes if you plan to use them sparingly. This is great if you can use a library, school, or work computer to do most of your research.

> *Use this phone when you call anyone concerning your escape plans, including possible rental properties, jobs, organizations, and even friends and family since your main cell phone conversations could be recorded.*

You can find plans that offer unlimited minutes, data, and texting for a low monthly cost of around $30. Or use an old phone you have, or buy a cheap phone where these plans are sold. They are sold at Target, Best Buy, Wal-Mart, Cricket, T-Mobile, Boost Mobile, and their websites.

Keep this phone hidden somewhere safe, in your desk at work or in a rented gym locker. If those aren't options, keep it at a friend or neighbor's house.

This may become your only phone if he cancels your main phone plan one day.

He mustn't find out this phone exists. So don't call or text anyone with this number who may tell him about it.

2. Use your work phone and email: While I don't recommend this, it's better than using your email and phone at home. It's cheaper than getting a burner phone and plan, and you don't have to worry about hiding it.

If your work phone is a cell phone and you're on call or expected to respond to calls or emails at random times, you probably take this phone into the house with you, which means your partner may go through this phone too.

Be careful if you use a landline at work and answer phone calls at your desk if you don't have a private office where you can close the door. You can expect everyone around you to hear your business.

They may gossip about you looking for a new place to live, and word can get back to your partner. Even if it's innocent, your coworker could blow your cover by making conversation with him: "So I heard you and Janice are looking for a new place to live."

Remember that your employer has the right and ability to monitor your business phone and computer activity. Will they care? Probably not, especially if personal use is minimal during work hours.

3. Use resources at a library, college, school, nonprofit, or friend's home: <u>This is nice because it's another free option.</u> You can make your own email address that you never access from your home or cell phone so he can't hack what he doesn't know exists.

The downside is that you likely won't have daily access to your info and any returned phone calls or texts. And if it's not your private phone line, it's also more complicated by burdening someone else to check it for you.

4. If you must use your own phone, laptop, or internet connection, follow the precautions below, especially if you don't have the money, resources, or ability to leave the house, or if you have good reason to believe he's not spying on you.

Don't leave a cookie trail—protect your internet history.

• Regularly clear cookies on your phone and computer. This erases your website history, making it less likely that recently visited website addresses will autocomplete if he starts typing in part of a word into the browser of a shared computer.

• Use the web browser's "private browsing" mode if possible. Chrome and Safari have this feature; other browsers may not. This will leave less internet history behind as it does not save cookies.

• Use a web browser you don't normally use. You can download a new one like DuckDuckGo or Firefox Mozilla. This is good because it won't autocomplete web addresses when he uses his usual browser. If you don't put it on the front page of your phone, it's not easily recognizable as a new download. Hide these apps within a larger cluster of apps so he doesn't notice it.

Create a different email address.

• Use a new email address in a new app. Choose a service that neither of you already have an email address with. Then download their app or use it in the web browser.

• If you download the app, don't use the email app you usually use. Hide this app in a folder that isn't on the first page of your phone.

• If you use the browser to access this email, use a different browser than usual and use the "private browsing" option.

• Make sure this password is totally different and not easy to guess. Set it so you need to input the password each time you log in to it.

• Create a new free email address on Google, Yahoo, Zoho Mail, Tutanota (encrypted), or Proton Mail (encrypted).

Camouflage contact names and delete texts and call logs.

• Delete any text messages or phone call records to places that involve your moving plans. But don't suddenly delete <u>all</u> your texts and phone calls, because this could be a red flag if you haven't done this in the past.

• Use aliases as contact names instead of real names in your contact list. If an apartment, women's shelter, or nonprofit calls and their real name pops up on caller ID, he may notice and become suspicious.

• <u>Note:</u> If you are on his cell phone plan, he can still get your call and text history from the carrier if he gets suspicious. But he can only see the times, dates, and numbers you texted with, not the content of the messages.

Download apps that offer a secondary phone number.

If you want to do it on the cheap but you are on his phone plan, this is a viable option. He won't be able to access your call and text logs through the cell phone carrier if you use this app instead of the regular calling and texting apps. And bonus, you don't have to buy a new phone.

• You will be assigned a second phone number. Your call and text record under this alternate phone number isn't available under your regular call and text list as you have to go into the app to see it.

• Make sure your phone is password protected and he doesn't know your password.

• Hide this app in another folder just in case.

• The downside of choosing this instead of a burner phone is if you're on a cell phone plan with him, he can still cut your phone service off.

• These apps work on both Apple and Android smartphones in the US: Google Voice (free), FreeTone (free with ads), TextFree (free with ads), Burner ($5/month for unlimited), Hushed (free trial, $5/month for unlimited), GoDaddy SmartLine (free trial, $10/month for unlimited).

While all of this is to keep his spying eyes away from your information, keep in mind that when you leave him, he will almost definitely end your cell phone plan if you're under his plan.

5. Get a backup phone: If you need a backup phone anyway, you might secure that phone before you leave. You will want to preemptively transfer your number to a new plan if you want to keep your old phone number because if he cancels your number before you've had a chance to transfer it, you will probably lose it forever and need a new phone number. This means that none of your old contacts will be able to contact you.

If your phone is locked to the carrier, try to get it unlocked ASAP because if he cancels your phone line before you unlock it, your phone will probably be useless. To use it again, you would need to pay off the rest of the old contract and sign your own contract with that same carrier. But you'll probably still lose your number. Your phone is probably locked if the carrier gave you a discount for signing a one- or two-year contract.

> **If you're not sure if it's locked or not, ask your phone carrier now.**

He may try to keep your phone or break it, especially if he paid for it. Back all your data, photos, and contacts up in the cloud and on your computer. Hopefully, he doesn't try to take your computer with your backup copy. Yet another reason it's vital to keep your plans top secret until you're already gone!

Another concern may be him tracking your location via your cell phone. If he doesn't turn your phone off, he still may be able to track your location. If he is tech savvy at all, you may want to turn your phone off and use your backup phone instead when you don't want to be found.

See more information about getting a backup phone in chapter 4.

Decide when to move

Generally, the sooner you leave the better.

> **If you are able to stay until you have ideal conditions for moving, then wait until he will be on a business trip or vacation. This is your window to move out, confrontation free.**

If he doesn't have any upcoming trips, you'll need to settle on a day when he's at work or gone most of the day.

If you need to save up some money or find a safe place to live, you can wait a few months—as long as you are physically safe living there.

Every situation is different. Some partners are super controlling and make living with them unbearable. Whereas, some are more absent and therefore bearable.

Don't stay just because you are hoping things work out with him and he will change for the better.

Reminder: He's already shown you his true colors. That is the real him. He's not gonna change, unless it's for the worse!

> Note: If he starts to show you any sign of physical abuse, leave immediately! This includes hitting, slapping, or shoving you. Forcibly taking items out of your hands and/or blocking you from leaving the house are also unacceptable. Doing any of these things to your pets or children is just as bad. Don't wait to save up money and get everything together.

Just get the basics and go—even if you have to stay in a shelter or on a friend's couch. Your safety and well-being are irreplaceable. If he starts getting physical, it will only escalate from there.

If he hides or steals your money or belongings without your permission, this is also a sign to leave as quickly as possible.

These behaviors reflect his moral code, which is extremely difficult to change, especially for a person who doesn't see it as a problem. You probably weren't the first woman he took his wrath out on, and won't be the last.

Story time:

I moved the majority of my stuff out while Vince was at his brother's wedding out of state. He expectedly disinvited me at the last minute. It was perfect because he was gone for days. I was able to pack everything myself. Then I hired a friend with a van to drive it to a different friend's storage unit an hour away.

When Vince returned, 90 percent of my stuff was gone. It would've been best if I left that weekend too. But I still had half a semester of teaching left and thought it would be easier to just stick it out living there for a few more months. In retrospect, I should've moved everything out and disappeared while he was out of state. I could've rented a short-term room near campus or stayed with a friend until I left for training.

When he asked about my missing stuff, I said I put it into storage. I said I did it for him, since he'd complained my stuff took up too much room. I don't know if he believed me. But he wanted to. He didn't say anything more about it.

The day I finally left didn't go smoothly because I gave him a heads up, so he purposely stayed at home all day. But I was still able to pack my little Honda with most of the remaining stuff I wanted to take and drive off.

Story time:

Things had gotten really bad with Josh. Most days Lisa couldn't even get out of bed. Luckily, her mom asked the right questions and was able to see that she was being abused.

One day while Josh was at work, Lisa asked her parents to drive down to help her move out. They put everything in boxes, loaded up her parents' SUV, and left. This only took them a few hours, with three people helping.

She said that everything fit into the little SUV because Josh made her get rid of most of her stuff before she moved in.

She also took her share of the money out of their joint bank account, then left town. He was clueless until he arrived home from work. Since he did freak out once he found out, it's a good thing she did it secretly and quickly! She and her dog got out safely and never looked back.

Lisa lived with her parents for almost a year while she recovered. She got a part-time restaurant job and saved up money. Within a year, she found a great job in her field, bought her own car, and moved into her own one-bedroom apartment.

~✎

How to decide what to pack

You want to prioritize packing and moving what is most important. Ask yourself, "If I run out of time toward the end, what belongings would be okay for me to leave and never see again?"

> **If you own lots of stuff, this will absolutely hamper your ability to move out.**

At the end of the day, being attached to your belongings can hold you back. Plus having a lot of stuff means it may take days to hire a moving truck to get your stuff out, making this an ordeal instead of a simple decision.

What to pack first

Go bag: Start with this. You always need a backpack or small duffel bag with a few changes of clothes, money, toiletries (toothbrush, toothpaste, soap, deodorant, lotion, lip balm, hair ties, etc.), extra medication, and important documents. You may want to leave this at work, in your rented gym locker, or in a trusted friend's house. Keep it in a place where he won't find it. Prepare this now so you'll have these essentials if he ever kicks you out temporarily, or if you decide to never return to the house to get the rest of your stuff. This is also good for if you get stuck in any emergency situation or evacuation.

Valuables and irreplaceable items: If something is very expensive, such as jewelry or rare coins, or a family heirloom your dead grandmother gave you, pack and move this stuff first. Take your expensive purses, sunglasses, and other pricey items with you now—especially if they don't take up much room.

Electronic equipment with your private data: This includes computers, tablets, e-readers, or anything else that would be costly to re-purchase. Plus, you don't want him to be able to retrieve data from it or give it to a pawn shop or to someone who would be able to take your private data off it. This is how identities can get stolen and people can get stalked.

Important documents and banking information: Keep these in a place where he can't access them. Hide your <u>original</u> passport, birth certificate, social security card, car title, contact numbers, prescriptions, and other information that's hard to replace. Copy front and back of replaceable cards, which will include the customer service numbers of credit or debit cards. He knows these items are important and can choose to take them at any time.

> <u>Note:</u> If for some reason he takes or hides your important documents, they are replaceable. It will just be annoying and costly. So don't lose hope if he won't give them to you.

What to pack second

Clothes you wear often: Many women keep too many clothes around, including stuff that we haven't worn in ages and doesn't even fit anymore. We typically cycle through and replace clothing, so it's all replaceable. But pack your favorites and move these after the important stuff.

Appliances, knick-knacks, decorations, etc.: Many of these are replaceable, take up lots of room, and aren't costly. If you don't have room, you can replace these later as you need to.

What to pack last

Pack these items only if you have ample time and space. Otherwise, leave them behind.

Older clothes and things you haven't used in a long time: While you may like to keep them, you won't miss them as much. You will survive without them. And probably not even want to replace them.

> Note: These old clothes are very useful for camouflaging your move. While you are packing the majority of your good clothes, you can put these old clothes out on the hangers to replace them. That way it doesn't look like your clothes are missing or disappearing.

Furniture: It's big and heavy to move. Plus, he's probably using it. He'll definitely notice if it suddenly goes missing.

Books, DVDs: Most are replaceable. This doesn't apply to signed, rare, or collector editions. You can replace these with digital ebooks later so you don't have to leave them behind every time you move. I've left so many books behind each time I've moved, and bought the same exact book more than once. Now I buy almost all ebooks instead of physical copies.

> Note: You can ship these separately via USPS under a much cheaper postage rate, classified as "media mail." This is reserved for books, DVDs, CDs. When you request this postage, you'll show the post office the box's contents before you seal and mail it.

Things you want to get rid of: Don't pack things you plan to throw out. If they are personal documents, take time to manually cut, burn, or shred them before you leave. If you or a friend have a yard, it may be easiest to burn these unneeded documents in a bonfire before you leave. Don't waste valuable packing space on trash. _It is vital to safely discard unneeded personal documents before you leave, so don't skip this step!_

Keep in mind that you may not be able to move everything out. This is why the order of packing and moving your belongings matters so much.

Some women in extreme circumstances won't be able to pack much. They may just pack a bag or two of essentials and need to leave very quickly. They may never see the rest of their stuff again. Prepare for this by moving your "pack first" items out now!

Pro tip: It's not always practical to move it all at once or hire a moving truck. If you have a lot of stuff and you plan to bring most of it, start packing little by *little. You can use your car or a friend's truck or van to drive it to a storage unit each week. If he notices, you can say that you're donating a lot of your stuff that you don't need anymore. You can also say that you are putting it in a (friend's) storage unit or relative's basement so the house isn't so cluttered. Say whatever makes the most sense in your situation.*

What to leave behind

If you have a ton of stuff that will take a long time to move or you're in a rush, you will need to think about what to leave behind.

Remember that furniture gets old, costs a lot to move, and can be replaced. Plus, it's very noticeable after it's gone. You don't want to do anything to raise his suspicions now. Unless the furniture is a family heirloom or valuable antique you can't live without, I'd recommend taking it last and only if you have time and space.

You can risk leaving a few things behind and hope he doesn't throw them away if you run out of time. If you could make him look bad and he cares about his professional reputation, or if he thinks you might come back, he might want to avoid making you mad by throwing your stuff away. A lot of this hinges on his morals, ego, maturity, and how you leave.

> **Just don't leave anything that you can't live without. Expect that he could get mad and throw it away.**

Story time:

I was lucky that Michael let me have my stuff back. Of course, he had incentive to keep it civil. He was up for tenure soon as a college professor and wanted to ensure nothing stopped him. He knew it wasn't beneath me to make a few phone calls to his boss about him. If his boss or department found out he had kicked me out into the streets with nowhere to go on a whim, his career would've been over. As a religious institution, they would've also been interested that he lied about his religion to get the job.

But with my relationship with Vince, I left some things at his house for different reasons. I had a hard deadline to be somewhere and ran out of time and space. I mainly left clothes and books. I told Vince I would come back to visit and was leaving for a job, <u>not because of him</u>. When he realized I wouldn't be back months later, he threw everything out. I did want my stuff and could've gone back for it. But I was too afraid to face him again.

> <u>Note:</u> Don't leave anything behind that would give him clues to where you are. This includes any important mail, keys, passwords, research notes, addresses, phone numbers, or documents that could give him access to any of your accounts or personal stuff.

What to do with your pets

Just like how your stuff can hamper you from moving out, pets can as well. Most rental and temporary places won't allow you to have pets. So see if a friend or family member can take care of your pet temporarily. This way you don't need to worry about them until you're in a stable living situation.

If you trust that he will care for your pet properly and will want to take care of them, you can leave your pet with him. Just don't expect that you'll be able to get the pet back in the future, if you take this option.

If you do leave your pet behind, don't let him dangle your pet as leverage so you'll talk to him, come visit, or live with him again.

Do not give him any clues that you are about to take your pet to live somewhere else. He will probably try to stop you, whether he likes your pet or not. Since he knows your pet is important to you, he may hold your pet hostage to keep you around.

> <u>Note:</u> Under no condition can you tell him who has your pet. You don't want a chance of him going to get the pet, or harassing your helpful friend.

Story time:

When I moved to California for graduate school, dogs weren't allowed in graduate student housing. So I couldn't take Chewy with me. Michael offered to take care of Chewy because he knew how important he was to me. He regularly sent me pictures of Chewy as an excuse to keep in touch, even though we were broken up.

When I left my program early, Michael convinced me to get back together and come live with him in New York. He knew I'd want to get my dog anyway, so it was harder to say no.

After reuniting with Chewy, he freaked out every time I left, barking and peeing all over the floor. He hadn't done that before, despite previously leaving him for several months with other family members. Chewy was never the same after living alone with Michael. So be careful who you trust your pets with.

Story time:

After I decided to leave Vince, who I dated after Michael, I called and researched many different apartments before moving out. But almost none of them allowed pets. Before I left for training, my longtime friend offered to take care of my dog. I knew she would be a great dog sitter because she grew up around dogs and is a caring and trustworthy human being. Her only condition was that I couldn't reveal to Vince who had my dog or where he was located. Her hunch that he might come looking for Chewy was spot on.

However, I made the mistake of telling Vince that I was giving Chewy to someone else so he should say goodbye. I said I was too busy working all the time now to regularly walk the dog. Therefore, I could no longer care for him properly. A sick friend of mine needed a companion, so I offered to give them Chewy temporarily. I told him that I thought he'd be happy since he always complained about him.

Even though he oftentimes acted like he hated the dog and viewed Chewy as a huge inconvenience to him, he secretly loved the dog. He blocked us from leaving the house and only stopped blocking the door after I convinced him that I had been kidding. I assured him I was just taking Chewy with me on a weekend trip, and that we would both be back soon. I hate to lie, but after my mistake in telling him, there was no other way out. My friend was already on her way, and I almost missed my train due to this delay.

My friend lived far away, so we met halfway to hand him off. Vince threw a fit when I returned without Chewy. But I was thankful that my dog was safe with someone I trusted, which is what mattered to me. My regret was that I hadn't done it sooner so I could've easily moved to a new apartment. I could've saved myself and Chewy from many months of unnecessary suffering.

Planning the logistics of moving your stuff

When figuring out what and how to pack and transport your stuff, ask these questions:

• How much stuff do you have?

• Are you using boxes, bags, or something else to transport it?

• Where are you moving your stuff—are you taking it directly to a storage unit, someone's home, your future home?

• Are you able to use your own vehicle or a friend's vehicle, or do you need to rent a UHaul truck, trailer, or van?

• Can you move everything yourself? Or do you need one–two friends to help? Are they reliable to show up at the agreed-upon time?

• Will you need to hire movers?

• Will you be moving it all in one shot? If not, how many trips back and forth will this take?

• Do you know his schedule or does he change it up and can come home at any time?

• Do you only have a six- to eight-hour window? Or can you do this over a few days while he's gone? If you know when he's going to be gone in the near future, this can help. As I've mentioned before, moving during his vacation or business trip is ideal.

See the budgeting funds section in chapter 3 for more details about considering costs.

ᵥᐟᐟᕲ

Do you need backup on move-out day?

You may need to consider having an escort help you move if

• You don't have a large chunk of time to move out while he's gone

• He has an unpredictable temper

• Just in case

Do as much as you can yourself. At no time did I ever bring a male friend to help me move anything. Even when I hired my friend with the van, he parked down the street and stayed in the vehicle. Vince was out of town, but he didn't want to be seen by the doorman or other neighbors. He said he didn't want Vince thinking he was my boyfriend, and responsible for me leaving Vince. So I packed and carried all the boxes out myself.

Why it's better to ask a female friend

If you have to go back to get stuff later, get a friend to pick it up for you or, at least, to accompany you. When deciding which friend to choose, you might think a male would be able to protect you better, especially if the situation gets physical and he either hits you or tries to restrain you from leaving, but really a female friend is the better option.

This is important because he won't feel competition or jealousy toward a female friend.

Somewhere in the back of his mind, he will wonder if the male friend convinced you to leave.

He may assume the guy is a romantic interest, even if it's not true. And if he wants to take his anger out on someone, most guys are more likely to punch another guy in the face versus a woman, so a female friend will reduce the chance of violence.

Choose someone who he already knows and gets along with, who can also appear to remain calm and neutral.

> Note: Don't bring a friend if there's any chance he will get violent toward a woman. You don't want to put her safety at risk. **You and your friends' life and health are not worth risking for belongings!** Rely on the police if you really need to get your stuff and you fear him.

Why calling the police can be useful

If you don't have an available friend or just want to pack alone, you can call the police to notify them.

> **Tell them you are moving out of your partner's house. Give them a heads up in case the guy won't let you leave, won't let you back in, or gets aggressive with you.**

This way you won't have to explain the entire situation to them if things get heated. They will be on standby and only come over if you call and tell them to.

<u>If your partner is prone to violence, you can always ask the police to come for the entire moving process.</u> They will usually come and watch to make sure you can leave okay—as long as it's not an all-day process.

> <u>Note:</u> If he is close with someone on the police force, only use this option if absolutely necessary.

> <u>Note:</u> If there are certain items or documents he won't hand over, the police may be able to make him hand them over if you know where he is hiding them. You can also return with the police at a later date to retrieve these items.

Where should you move to?

Don't let his bad behavior rush you into big commitments or big decisions.

If he's acting out, it can feel like torture. And you'll do anything to get away from it. But be careful, and don't make a rash decision you'll regret later.

> **Realize the first place you move to is only temporary. It's best to move into a place that doesn't require a long lease or contract.**

That way you don't have to rush into making a big commitment you may regret in two months. <u>Then once your mind is clear and you're living on your own terms, you can make long-term decisions.</u>

<u>Story time:</u>

Some days I could barely stand my living situation. It felt like the mental torment would never end; I just wanted to move out as quickly as possible. But since I had signed up for the military, I couldn't leave until training started. So I called to ask my recruiter if he could possibly move up my training schedule.

I was ready to go enlisted rather than as an officer—a contract for a four-year position earning a fraction of the salary and lower living standards. Luckily, he told me there were no earlier openings available to me. He saved me from making a rash decision that wouldn't have benefited me.

Maybe you're not sure where to go yet. Do you want to stay local? Or get as far away as possible? Deciding to stay in your own town or not can be a tough decision.

Staying nearby

Maybe you've always lived in the same hometown and you don't want to leave. This can be good because chances are you have a lot of supportive friends and family nearby who can help you out.

Some other benefits for saying local include:

• Can stay with friends or family for a short time while you look for another permanent place to live.

• Can easily find roommates you already know.

• Can split the rent and save money.

• Can enjoy the company and benefit from the positive environment.

• Have people nearby who care about you and can talk some sense in to you if you get lonely or sad and want to go back to him.

• Can keep your same job.

• Will be near your support system.

The <u>cons</u> of staying local include:

• He will know you are still around.

• You may bump into him at the grocery store or anywhere else.

• He can stalk you if he finds out where you move to or if he knows where you work.

• He may spread bad rumors about you. It's easy to get pulled back into the drama.

• Mutual friends may take sides and treat you differently.

• You have a lot of reminders of him around, so it's easier to fall into the trap of getting back together. He's conveniently right there when you feel lonely.

• You won't get a fresh start.

If you stay local, just make sure it is at least thirty minutes away from your current place.

That way it drastically cuts down on the chances that he'll see you. He's less likely to drive by and see your parked car in the driveway or you out in the yard.

Moving far away

If you want to venture farther, this can be the chance and excuse you've been waiting for. You can get a fresh start somewhere else in a different environment so you can feel different. You'll never have to see him or reminders of the places you used to go together, helping you put him out of sight, out of mind, which really works. And you will get over the relationship quicker.

If you leave town, think of where you may want to go. You don't need to stay there permanently if you aren't sure.

> **If you start stressing about this decision, remember, *nothing needs to be permanent.***

There's a good chance you'll be living in a different place a year or two after you leave your partner anyway.

Since the move can be stressful, you want to keep it simple. The simpler you make this first move, the more likely it is to be successful-- especially since you are doing it quickly and secretly.

Some ideas for the move:

• Leave town for several months to work somewhere else; you can always move right back if you miss your town.

• Move two hours away and quickly find an hourly job there. Then spend time looking for a better job in another state. That way you don't have to make a big move right away.

• Temporarily stay with a friend or family member who lives in a town you like while you look for a job and your own place.

• Use the time to travel for a bit before you decide where to settle down.

• Join the military.

Traveling as an option

Maybe you're not sure where you want to move next, or you don't want to commit to moving to an area before finding a job there first.

In that case, you can go couch surfing with friends, live in hostels, or find a job on a cruise ship. These are all options to get out of town for a while, especially if you're not sure where you want to live next. This may also be the safest option if you're afraid he'll follow you.

You will need to put all your stuff into a storage unit or leave it with a friend until you return.

> *If you don't have a place in mind, you can head to seasonal vacation destinations during the tourist season, such as a theme park like Disney World during the summer or a mountain ski resort in the winter.*

These places always hire a ton of people just before the season starts. These jobs are also fun and temporary. The new mental stimulation will get your mind off of what you left.

Don't worry too much about the location as you're not signing up for any long-term commitments or putting roots down. You'll be ready to move to the next place to explore and do something else if you choose to.

Should you really join the military?

If you don't know what to do next, you may consider joining the military. The military is an awesome option, and many people end up joining because they are trying to get out of a bad situation they're in. If you are under 40, it's easy to join the enlisted ranks as long as you don't have documented health or mental health issues. If you have a college degree, you can apply to be an officer. If you have a specialized skill like nursing, you can be over 40 to join.

They give you a salary, paid training, free health care, free college, built-in friends, and a place to live. And a fresh start in a new city. They take care of all the planning and decisions for you. All you need to do is take an entrance exam and choose a job. Sounds great, right?

> **The only problem is, you will be attracting abusers wherever you go right now until you've detoxed and healed from this relationship.**

So while you are fragile, it's best to surround yourself with people you trust, not drill instructors who are going to scream in your face and potential toxic classmates who may throw you under the bus in order to make themselves look better. These screaming men can easily trigger a lot of trauma, especially if the partner you're leaving is a yeller.

Focus on finding a place to stay and recover for at least six months. The military and boot camp will still be there later.

Plus, once you've spent time away from him, you'll be thinking more clearly. You don't want to jump into signing a contract now and regret it later. Once you sign, you're committed to three–six years. You can't change your mind later without getting a bad discharge.

So you need to plan it right and go in with a stable and strong mindset.

<u>Story time:</u>

I joined the military to leave a guy. In the beginning of boot camp, I froze or sometimes cried anytime someone yelled at me. I felt so triggered and frightened. Because I gave off every codependent signal in the book and they could sense I was used to being bullied, some staff labeled me as weak and an easy target. I got mercilessly bullied for months. They took my codependent signals as permission to treat me the same. They thought I wouldn't do anything to fight back. They figured if they treat me the same as everyone else, I'm already used to it.

Eventually, I straightened out and got used to all the yelling and games. I excelled, especially for an older woman training with guys a foot taller and decade younger than me. Aside from an injury that slowed me down a bit, I became class president and one of the strongest candidates.

But it didn't matter by then. I was already labeled, and many people don't like to change their opinions and first impressions of others. In the military, there is nothing more important than giving a positive first impression and the ability to blend in with everyone else.

Image is much more important than anything else. Competency, skills, and intelligence are very secondary.

If I could go back in time, I would never have jumped into boot camp directly after leaving a bad relationship. That's why I recommend taking time to rest and heal first. But I would do it again if I didn't have a choice in the timing.

> **Even though my boot camp experience was extra harsh, it's one of my most life-changing events. My military experiences cured my codependency and gave me strength and bulletproof confidence.**

I would highly recommend eventually joining the military to anyone who wants to learn new skills, move their career forward, travel, and grow as a person.

Types of housing

Depending on where you live, you have different options and price points. There will be tradeoffs between cost, convenience, speed of move-in, and lease lengths. I've divided them into categories based on these factors.

> Note: If you don't own a car, remember that you'll need to live near a bus or subway system route. If public transportation isn't available, live within walking or biking

distance to major stores, potential employers, and other places you'll want to go.

Easy, cheap, convenient, probably fast, likely no deposit

House sitting: Several websites connect sitters with homeowners who only live somewhere seasonally and who want someone to live in their home while they're away for several months at a time. Duties may include watering plants and taking care of pets. If you have relatives or family friends who have a seasonal home, you can ask them directly if they need a house sitter. Sometimes people would like a house sitter but don't advertise it because they don't want a stranger in their home.

> *Typically home owners pay you or let you stay there for free. You'll need to leave eventually, but at least you'll have a few weeks or months of downtime and free rent to make plans.*

Renting a room in a friend's house: Do you have any friends in the area who own a house with extra bedrooms? Are they stable and someone you'd like to live with? Ask them if they'll rent a room to you.

Staying with a romantic partner: I included this section only to tell you it is *not* an option you should consider. Please don't move in with a guy. You don't want to get trapped in a cycle with someone else. Anyone can seem nice at first, especially when you compare them to your current situation, where your partner has already revealed his true self.

> **When you are emitting a frequency of sadness, dependence, desperation, fear, or anything negative, you won't be attracting anyone good, much less the partner of your dreams.**

I know he may offer you a free place to stay and may even say it's temporary to lure you in. But this is how you get trapped—and dependent on someone else again.

The most important thing for you to do right now is break this unhealthy pattern of depending on someone else. You need to break free and become financially independent.

> **When you are financially independent, no one owns you or can question or control what you do in your own life.**

You may not even realize how stifled you are right now, until you're out.

Story time:

Things were getting very bad with Michael. I'd taken breaks a few times because it was too unbearable to stay with him. I'd stay with other friends, including my friend who'd become increasingly obsessed with me, Vince.

Deep down, I knew that it wasn't a good idea to move in with another man right away. I even told Vince that when he asked me to move in with him.

So while I told him no initially, rent in New York was super expensive and I had no job at the time. Most places also didn't allow dogs, so I felt stuck. Vince kept offering his place. Finally, Michael kicked me out of the house on a whim, so I ended up living with Vince by default, because I had no job or plan. Big mistake.

Within a few months, my life went from fairytale to nightmare. I'd realized I'd made a huge mistake by moving in with someone just as bad. My friend had tried to warn me: "Better the devil you know than the one you don't."

Toxic people can sense when you've been eating poison somewhere else, and they plan to keep feeding it to you.

If you are already with one toxic guy, chances are the guy you meet while you're with him or soon after will be just as toxic, if not worse. You are very low energy right now and so attracting other low-vibe people.

Trust me, you will not meet a healthy man at this stage in your life until you heal. He may seem like your fairytale knight in shining armor, but that's just because anything looks great compared to the current guy! Especially when you're only seeing the new guy's public, perfectly crafted persona.

And if he is already offering you a place to stay and other perks? Just run. You don't want a repeat of what just happened. All you need to do is focus on recovering from the current guy. Not subjecting yourself to the same experience again.

Staying with a family member: Do you have any family members in the area who have an extra room or who are living in a city you want to live in? Offer them some money to live in their extra room for a while. This way they don't feel like you owe them anything or that they can control you. Just be sure they are dependable. You don't want them changing their mind last minute. Also, make sure they are positive people. The last thing you need right now is someone criticizing and rehashing all the mistakes you already know you made.

Takes longer to find, has an application process and some restrictions, not guaranteed, but cheap

Renting a room in a larger house or apartment: If you already know someone, this is ideal. But you can also look on Craigslist. There are always people looking for roommates or for someone to rent out a spare room.

Single women's dorms (available in larger cities): These are typically large houses where women can rent a bedroom for a fraction of the price it would cost to rent anywhere else. They usually share common areas, such as a kitchen and bathroom, with other tenants.

There will be rules, such as a minimum number of hours you need to work, volunteer, or go to school. So you may need to have something lined up before moving in. They may have specific age requirements and probably won't allow pets, guests to stay over, or men. This last rule may be a good one to keep you out of trouble, for now.

Renting a room with a senior citizen (available in larger cities): In some larger cities with high rent, you can find matching services to match seniors with a roommate. This is mainly so the seniors can stay in and afford their homes. New York City has this, and it can make an otherwise unaffordable city, affordable.

This application process can take weeks or months while they look for an appropriate match and set up meetings.

> *But the fewer conditions you have, such as a higher budget, no pets, no gender preference, and larger geographical area, the faster they can find a match.*

More privacy, more expensive, has an application process, longer wait time, locked into a lease or mortgage, deposit or down payment:

A lot will be changing for you in a short amount of time after you move out. If you want to be free to move to another area for a job, school, adventure, or another great opportunity; are ready to sign a year-long commitment; and can buy a bunch of furniture and supplies, then these options are for you.

Renting your own apartment: This will typically require you to sign a year-long lease; otherwise, you'll pay a much higher rate. They may also call your current housing or landlord to ensure you are up to date with rent. Be ready to provide a reference's name who isn't connected to your partner. You wouldn't want to write down your partner's name and have them calling him or his landlord.

You will probably need to buy all your own bedroom and living room furniture, in addition to kitchen appliances, dishes, and cooking ware. And then box it all up and hire moving trucks when you're ready to leave.

Buying a home or condo: Keep in mind you will have many expenses that come with a new house, such as inspections, costs of new appliances, equipment, and repairs—in addition to the furniture and supplies costs of renting your own apartment. Buying a permanent home keeps you tied to a certain area and also ties you down with fixed payments.

Very fast, but can get expensive in the long term:

AirBnB: It's free to sign up for this. You can see tons of listings for the city you list. You can stay in one place long term or go all over the world. Or you can stay as short as one–three days, a few weeks, or even work out a longer deal with the landlord privately if you get along and want to stay. Most places give a discount if you stay at least three days. You can leave on short notice or stay a very long time. Since these are in residential areas, you can use this service to check out different cities or neighborhoods to sample what area you would like to live in more permanently.

You won't need to pay a deposit and furniture and clean linens are included. Often there is a full-sized kitchen you can use, and if you're lucky, there's even some tea and little snacks included. Other guests or even hosts may stay there. So you can meet and talk to other interesting people. This will help keep your mind off him and curb loneliness.

Extended Stay Hotels: You usually pay for this weekly without needing to make a deposit. It includes all furniture, linens, electricity, water, and internet. Additionally, they often have a kitchen and full-size refrigerator, where you can store and prepare your own meals. You can get up and move elsewhere with little notice. It's usually much cheaper than a nightly hotel room rate.

Very fast, free, or cheap:

Town welfare: Some towns have rules on the books to house you somewhere if you find yourself homeless and don't have resources. They will ask for proof of your financial information, so be ready for this. They may place you in a hotel, rooming house, or shelter.

Churches: Sometimes they'll let you live there or stay in exchange for working there, especially if you tell them your situation. They are also an excellent resource, as they may have families in the community looking to rent out an extra room in their home and often have ties to nonprofits with who they can connect you with. They often have a fund to help people in need, such as those in your situation.

Shelters: They have women's and domestic violence shelters. This can be good if you think your ex is dangerous—as in he might come looking for you and stalk you, hurt you, threaten you, or just harass you. They usually hire guards who are trained for these situations and know how to keep exes out.

While you may be able to show up that day, call ahead, just to be sure that they aren't full for the night.

Storage unit: If you're on a super tight budget or run out of time, you can always spend the night in the storage unit with your stuff.

Car: If you are in a bind, sleeping in your car for a few nights is always an option. I've done this while traveling to save money. Designated rest stops and Walmarts are good for this because they have restrooms, people around, and often security guards. If you do this for more than a couple of days, you can use a friend's house or gym to shower.

Remember that these options where you don't have your own room are for the short term only. You don't want to get stuck in homelessness; otherwise, you'll be more tempted to go back to him.

> <u>Note:</u> None of these options need to be permanent, especially if you are not signing a lease. You can change your mind in a few months or even a few days. The beauty of it is that you can move quickly or upgrade once you get a better job. So don't get decision fatigue over it. Just think about what options are in your budget and seem easiest for you right now. Start there.

Chapter 2 review

What to be aware of as you plan

• You don't want him to find out what you're doing.

• Be careful about using your own smartphone, computer, or home internet connection to make your plans to leave.

• He could bug the house, install spyware on your phone or computer, monitor internet traffic, look at your phone statement call and text history, or know your phone's password and go through it.

• He may come home early and overhear your phone conversations if you talk in the house.

• Your best bet is to do your research at a library, friend's house, or other WiFi hotspot like a coffee shop.

• If you can afford it, your best bet is to have a burner phone to do your research and make phone calls. Hide it somewhere he can't get to. *This is a must if you are on his cell phone plan.*

• If you must use your own phone, at a minimum, delete the call log, internet browser history, and text messages that might give away your plans. Use a private browser.

• If you're on his phone plan, be ready for him to turn off the phone immediately after you leave.

When to move

• How soon can you have the money to leave? Sooner is better.

• Caveat: If he's physically abusive at all, don't wait until you have the money, the time is now.

• If you can, wait for a time when he'll be out of town or, at least, gone all day.

• If he's gone for several days, you can pack and move all your stuff out over that period.

• If he's gone for only one day at a time, you may need to pack and move your stuff out little by little, under the guise that you are donating clutter to clear space.

What to pack

• Prioritize what you pack and load first, in case you run out of room or need to leave stuff behind.

• The first things you pack should be your go bag, valuables and irreplaceable items, electronic equipment with your private data, your official passport and identification, and extra copies of important documents and banking information.

• The second things you should pack are the clothes you wear often, your appliances, knick-knacks, decorations, etc.

• The last things you should pack, and may even consider leaving behind, are your older clothes and things you haven't used in a long time, furniture, books, DVDs, and things you want to get rid of.

What to do with your pets

• Consider asking a trusted friend or family member to take care of your pet until you're in a stable living situation. This way it's one less worry, and your partner can't hold your pet hostage.

• Don't let your partner know the location or person who is taking care of your pet.

Logistics of moving your stuff

• Think about the amount of stuff you have and what you're packing it in.

• Have a location to store your stuff: Are you taking it directly to your new place, a friend's house, or a storage unit?

• What vehicle are you using to transport your stuff: Your own car, rented truck, or moving company?

• How many people do you need to move it?

• Multiple trips or one shot: Do you have time to make multiple trips to move your stuff?

• What is your time window for moving while he's away.

Do you need to ask for help on move-out day?

• Consider this option if: You don't have enough time when he leaves to move, he has a bad temper, just in case.

• You can bring a friend to help and observe, preferably a female. Don't put your friend at risk if your partner is violent.

• You can call the police. They can either be in standby mode to come if you need them, or they can supervise your quick move out.

Where to move

• Local: cheaper, more convenient, social support.

• Farther away: fresh start, a new adventure safely away from him.

• If you want to escape, go on an adventure, or just take longer to decide your next move, then consider traveling for a time.

• The military can be a great option for self-development, career, fun, and travel—but wait six months or longer. This commitment isn't something to rush into. You need to rest and recover before making this life-changing decision, and before heading to boot camp.

Different types of housing

• Options for differing levels of housing include cheap, fast, convenient, very short term.

• Start with considering friends, family, and contacts, but do not move in with a romantic or potential romantic partner.

• Renting is best for now, especially if you don't need to sign a year-long lease.

• Now isn't a time for long-term buying decisions.

National Domestic Violence Hotline: Why is Escalation so Dangerous? https://www.thehotline.org/resources/escalation/.

CHAPTER 3

Budgeting Expenses and Procuring Money

W E NEED TO CONSIDER your finances if you have a tight budget. To do this, we need to first note how much money you currently have and ways you can get more money.

Budgeting secretly

Does he know how much money you have?

If he knows the amount of money you have, he'll think he has the upper hand. Since he knows how long you can go without finding a job if you don't get other funds, he can start trying to lure you back when he estimates you'll need money again.

If you're not married, I recommend never revealing this amount to a man. Or anyone else for that matter. It's none of their business, and there's no benefit to giving away this private information.

> **Even if you are married, you should always keep a separate account with only your name on it.**

This way, you'll always retain some control of your life, regardless of your spouse's hidden intentions.

If he asks you directly how much money you have, what should you say? Not the real number. Either lie or say it's none of his business.

> **If you have trouble withholding personal information from nosy questioners, you need to get over this. This is how abusers take advantage of you in relationships and in life.**

How secure is your personal savings account?

Many controlling partners make you deposit your money into a joint account, or one they can access. They may also try to monitor and control your spending.

If he has access to your money, you are going to need to move it into a different account. <u>If you simply take his name off, he can still access it if he has the account number, debit card, PIN number, checkbook, or account passwords.</u>

So you need to change your passwords, PIN number, and account number. If you cancel the account altogether, this may raise his suspicions if he's keeping tabs on it. Just move the bulk of the money to an account he doesn't know about for now. Withdraw the cash or do this through a cashiers' check or money order. <u>If you directly transfer the money to the new account, he may be able to trace it or recall the money if he can access it.</u>

<u>Note:</u> Don't have any financial information mailed to your house or stored there. This is a good time to go paperless and have the statements sent to an email address he doesn't have access to. It's also a good time to put a different address as your home address. You don't want him to find your new account numbers and information, or you're back to square one!

We'll cover more details on how to set up your own account and private mailbox in chapter 4.

<u>Story time:</u>

Vince and I always kept separate accounts and did not mix finances. That is, until he found out my checking account number and started paying his credit card bills out of my account without my permission. My banker was supportive and said he often sees this type of theft between estranged family members and partners. He suggested I file a police report so I could press charges and get all the money back.

Unfortunately, I'd recently started my job and felt I didn't have enough money to move out yet. So I couldn't risk upsetting him by doing the police report. I also knew he would be pissed when his payments from my account didn't go through. So I played dumb and told him that my banker said "someone" stole my identity and I should press charges. I also said I was stressed because my account was overdrawn, and I might have to pay a bunch of fees for that. That last part wasn't true, but Vince was starting to get upset about his cards not getting paid off. Once I mentioned the banker pressuring me about the police report, fees, and the overdrawn account, he became silent.

I don't think he actually needed my money. I think he just planned to drain my bank account so I wouldn't have the resources to move to my own place. *This* *didn't happen again, because I put my foot down. I also explained the situation without blaming him, but instead pinned it on an "unknown person" who overdrew my account. That way it didn't trigger his ego.* **Mentioning the police and banker's support helped because it showed I had people in my corner and knew my legal rights. Plus, I focused on the stressful situation that my account was overdrawn, and didn't directly accuse him.** *He was also satisfied because he (mistakenly) thought I had no money left, therefore, no funds to leave.*

I felt a crippling amount of fear when I went home to tell him what happened. But due to the way I framed the situation, he thought he gained valuable insight about my lack of funds and saw it as a win. This knowledge put him in a good mood, and I avoided seeing a meltdown despite the fact that most of the payments got canceled.

⤙⊱

Does he pay your bills directly or give you a set allotment?

How your bills get paid now will help you decide: 1) when and what to cut back on and 2) when and how to save your money.

If he's directly paying off your credit card every month, go ahead and keep buying these things for now. Just be sure to cut them out once you leave and are paying out of your own pocket.

But if it's coming out of a set allotment he gives you each month, stash the difference into a separate bank account that he doesn't know about and can't access. Do not feel guilty.

Anything you purchase with a joint credit card, he will be able to see. This includes stores, dates, and locations. This may give him information about your plans. So don't start buying new kitchen supplies quite yet. But if you are buying gift cards for your friend's birthday, anniversary, or other holiday, this isn't too suspicious. Wink.

> *Pro tip: If you're tight on moving expenses, you can use a credit card he pays for to buy gift cards for future housing appliances. Target, Walmart, and Bed Bath & Beyond come to mind. (Don't feel bad if he can afford it. He is the one driving you out!)*

The many ways to get more funds

Ideally, you want to get enough funds to move and pay for three months of living expenses.

Don't feel daunted by this or feel that it's not doable. Don't fall into the trap of using this as an excuse to stall your big move. Also do not depend on funds from him in a divorce. You will likely get some alimony—eventually. But don't count on getting payments for the first year or few. During this time, he will stall.

> **He's hoping you will give up, give in, and go back to him, or let him off without making him pay. Taking him to court and getting what you deserve can take a long time, even if your lawyer does her job properly.**

There are different ways to handle this. You don't need to procure all the money at once. *The money can come from different places—both expected and unexpected.* Let's get creative!

Should you find a job now or not?

At this point, it's best to not worry about finding a job if you don't have one already. Just focus on leaving safely.

You can *passively* look for a new job if you plan on staying in the same town. Think about places he would not frequent, such as areas of town he doesn't usually go to. But I wouldn't actually spend the time applying now.

If you want to start working soon after leaving, you can get a job and start working very quickly. Think low-hanging fruit—easy to find and get. You can take this as a stepping stone while you continue to look for a better-paying professional job or work your way up at the company.

> Note: You are not in the best mindset to search for a great job right now. Since you are in a rocky position, you may not be able to focus and perform your best. You want to be able to concentrate and bring your best self to your dream job so you don't jeopardize your future there.

With that said, if you're in desperate need of money right now, you may have no choice; just make sure you are depositing this money in your own bank account that he can't access (see chapter 4 for more details about setting up a personal, secret bank account).

> *If he takes away your money or tries to sabotage your job, there's no point in working until you're out.*

If you must get a job now, try to find a job where you get paid in cash. If you desperately need to make some quick money, get a job that pays tips out every day. These jobs also get you working quickly. They are usually hospitality jobs, such as:

• waiting tables at a restaurant

• working at the coat check in a club

• working as a car valet

If you have no restaurant experience, you may have trouble finding a job waiting tables. But you can start as a hostess or bus girl—just ask ahead if these positions also receive a tip out each day. And with this job, if you have to quit suddenly or take time off, it's not a huge deal, especially if it's a large restaurant. These places usually have a large staff and high turnover anyway, and other employees willingly pick up your extra shifts.

> *If you are cute and have a bubbly personality, this is a bonus in a customer-facing, tip-dependent position.*

If you can't find a cash-paying job, try out these jobs:

Substitute teaching: These positions usually aren't competitive, and there's no lengthy interview or waiting process. They are usually desperate for people since it can be high stress and they don't pay much. If you've been out of the job market for a while or have school-aged kids, this is a good option. They do a simple criminal and educational background check. To know what you will be paid, check out the pay scale as it depends on your educational attainment. And since they post new jobs daily, you can decide which ones to take or not. This is good because while you are busy moving, you can simply not accept jobs for those days. If you move out of the immediate area, you can just stop taking jobs altogether, without putting in a resignation or feeling loyalty to the job.

Temp agencies: Temporary agencies are good because they place you at different places that need someone with your skills. You interview once with them and maybe take some skills tests, such as typing. Then they do the rest of the work for you, instead of you taking the time to look for jobs. And luckily, you can accept only shorter-term jobs if you know you'll need to take time off to move. Meanwhile, you're easing your way back into the job market and making new connections. Your confidence in the workplace will increase, and you'll figure out what type of job you want long term.

It may be nice to get out of the house too. This will take up a significant amount of time. Just don't let this throw you off track for your plans.

Which of your skills can you earn money from?

If you have a specific skill, you can offer your services. Skills such as

• Cooking

• Gardening

• Cleaning houses

• Shoveling snow or snow blowing

• Mowing the lawn

• Cleaning cars

• Pet sitting

• Bathing or grooming dogs

• Baby sitting

• Tutoring kids

You can do these things for neighbors for extra cash. Or better yet, go to a wealthy neighborhood and ask around, knock on doors, or pass out flyers.

> *Someone probably needs the help, and you'll be doing them a huge favor. They will likely pay you above the market rate for the convenience of you coming to their house.*

This way they don't need to take time out of their day to drive somewhere. This will also get you out of the house.

Story time:

Naomi escaped Canada as a young adult to get away from her abusive and overbearing father, and the conservative community he controlled. She landed in New York City.

Since she was illegally in the country, she couldn't get a job. She needed a place to stay and come with almost no money. Although she is Jewish, she lived at a Hare Krishna house for free while pretending to buy into their beliefs. She only had to do a few chores for them in exchange, such as cooking, cleaning the house, and singing with them in subway stations.

She printed business cards for her own dog-walking business and went to dog parks near wealthy neighborhoods to meet people and hand them out. From this, she got several dog-walking clients and would walk three–five dogs at a time.

Within a few months, she was able to move out of the Hare Krishna house and afford a nice one-bedroom apartment in Manhattan. A few years later, she'd saved up enough money to buy her own two-bedroom condo in Manhattan. She said she never meant for it to be a career, but the money was too good to stop. She also boasted about how she worked less than eight hours a day, and would never make this kind of money using her college degree. She earned much more money walking dogs independently than she would working for a company that keeps most of the profits.

꩜

Which of your belongings are profitable to sell?

Do you own stuff you don't use or need? After all, you probably want to limit the belongings you take with you when you move. The more you have, the more time it'll take. It's also more expensive to move and store it. Look around and see if you have any expensive items you don't use anymore. Expensive means they still have a high resale value. Focus on the things you can get a lot of value from quickly.

Any items that are unused and still have tags on them, try to find the receipts and return them if you don't need them. Even if it's past the return window, many places may offer a merchandise credit. Even if it's not cash, it can still save you precious space when you're moving.

Designer clothes, shoes, purses: Worn clothes usually don't retain their value. You can give them to friends, donate them, or try to sell them. While you can donate them to the Salvation Army or another thrift shop for a future tax write-off, note that they don't pay cash. Consignment stores may try to help you sell very nice pieces. *You can list pieces on phone apps like Poshmark, which sells secondhand clothing and accessories directly to consumers; it's similar to eBay.* Secondhand stores like Plato's Closet will give you a small amount of cash for recent fashion styles. *If you have new clothes with tags still on them and a receipt, try to return them first. Even if it's beyond the return window, many will offer you a gift card.*

Jewelry: Don't take this to a pawn shop or places that pay per pound of gold. They will rip you off. Instead, your best bet is to sell it to a direct buyer. But it may not be worth it if you will lose a lot of money and they don't pay what it's worth.

Rare coins or precious metal bars: If you research the value online yourself, you can either sell it online or take it to a trusted precious metals dealer. You should be able to get very close to the retail value of what these valuables are worth.

Inherited items: If you inherited property, a vehicle, collector's items, or other big-ticket items, now might be the time to sell them if they are just sitting around unused. Right now, ask yourself if the sentimental value or the cash value would be more useful to you.

> <u>Note:</u> Don't take lowball offers out of desperation. Research online and try to get market value. Never take it to a pawn shop, and never tell buyers that you really need the money soon. Ask a minimum of three or four different buyers for offers.

If you're still short on cash, don't despair. There are other places you can get money.

If he gives you cash, save it!

How to get and hide extra cash from him

Use a debit card linked to his account to make purchases at the grocery store, drug store, pharmacy, or anywhere else that gives cash back: Take out a reasonable amount of cash to use for "legitimate expenses." Try to go to a place that you regularly make lots of purchases from, so it doesn't look suspicious. Choose the maximum amount of cash back that won't attract attention. Use your discretion—get anywhere between $20 to $100.

Use an ATM card to withdraw cash: Only do this if you have his permission and preferably your own name is on the card too. Try to mirror his ATM patterns if you know it. For example, if he takes out $200 per week on Fridays, do the same. If he goes every Monday and Friday and withdraws $100 each time, do that. Remember, they do have cameras at ATM machines, so don't do this if he'll get mad at you for using the card.

Ask him for cash: Spend most of it on legit expenses, whether it's clothes, groceries, or medicine, but then keep some for yourself.

Regularly and quickly deposit this money into a personal bank account he doesn't know about: Try to do this daily, or whenever you get more than $50. This makes it less likely he'll find your getaway money if it's in your purse or pockets. (If you don't already have your own bank account, see chapter 4 on how to go about this.)

Note: Be ready with a simple explanation if he asks you what you spent the money on. Don't get nervous. Just keep your cool and act normal. If you go into too many details, you'll raise his suspicions. Don't bring it up unless he asks you directly.

You can find clever places to hide your money before you make it to the bank.

Story time:

Mary married a narcissist and had two kids with him. She waited until their kids graduated high school to leave him. He made a high income as a software engineer, and she was a stay-at-home mom.

She said she started saving a bit of the money he gave her each week and hid the extra cash somewhere he wouldn't look. Her favorite place? Feminine pads. She opened the pad, put the (100) dollar bills inside, then re-folded and re-sealed the pad.

And he never caught her.

Over a five-year period, she took out $20,000 and hid it in her own secret bank account. She also took half of the money out of their joint checking account right before she filed for divorce. This money is enabling her to live comfortably while he dilly-dallies about signing the divorce paperwork and paying her any alimony. Not knowing she has this extra money, he thinks he can starve her out by taking a long time to sign the papers. He's counting on her running out of money and giving in to his lowball offer of not splitting their property fairly. But it won't work due to her secret stash.

Throughout the marriage, he always questioned her about her expenses and regularly went through her purse and other belongings. But thanks to her feminine pads, she was still able to pull this off!

How to leverage programs designed to help you

A lot of this will depend on the city you're in. Larger cities tend to have more resources and funds. But you can find many special programs and resources for those affected by domestic violence nearly anywhere. While you may not want to label yourself as a domestic violence victim because you may not think of your situation as that severe, if you are in a relationship where your financial dependence is keeping you with someone who is bad for your mental well-being, you qualify.

Many of these resources and nonprofits aren't advertised or easy to find. That's why you need to connect with a good local social worker to find out about them.

Social workers: Find a social worker to help you navigate your options, including local programs and nonprofits. Be sure it's someone you feel comfortable with who takes her job seriously and actually wants to help you. Keep looking until you find the right one. It's worth it because they are a wealth of knowledge. They're not only trained for this but they also have professional connections to these places and have experienced the ins and outs of how these programs operate and know your realistic options.

You can find a social worker at a women's shelter. You can also call 211 or the National Domestic Violence Hotline at 1-800-799-233. Both take calls 24/7 and will connect you to local help and resources.

Churches: Every church has resources to help those who are down on their luck. Most have a food pantry and even a fund that helps people with bills. This can include one-time rent payments.

The food pantry is usually open during a specific time and date each week or by appointment. This can help if you run out of food and have a limited budget. If you tell them it's an emergency, they are more likely to help sooner. Don't be bashful. This exists to help people like you.

The best place to go for this is straight to the church leader. Set up a meeting with them. You can speak to them after church or call to set it up. It is best if you can do it when you have privacy and they aren't distracted. That way they can focus their attention on you, without rushing off to do something else.

> *Pro tip: You can call the administrative office to ask, but sometimes for them, it's just a job. I've called many churches to coordinate events, and sometimes the receptionist just tries to get rid of the call and do the least amount of work possible. Some don't have the same passion that the church leaders do, and simply don't care enough to take the extra effort. If I call the same church and speak to the leader, they are often way more welcoming and available to help.*

If you feel bad about taking charity, you can offer to pay them back or volunteer your time once you become fully independent again.

Government programs: Government programs are another option that's available in some form or another in all developed countries. The downside is, it can be a slow process. In fact, you might need to wait a couple of months before they process your application. If you let them know you are in an emergency situation, they may be able to expedite your money.

While the rules and exact amounts vary depending on the state you live in, they all have income and savings thresholds that you need to fall below. Chances are that you'll be eligible for more money and programs if you have minor children. *A social worker can help you apply for all these programs and make it much easier for you.*

Food stamps: This is also known as SNAP (Supplemental Nutrition Assistance Program) in the US. You receive a reloadable debit card with a certain amount each month that you can only spend on food. While single adults can qualify for food stamps, there is usually a work requirement after the first few months if you have no minor children. Exact qualifications and dollar amounts vary by state. You can find more information on your state's SNAP website or from your social worker.

Cash assistance: This is usually only for adults who have minor children. This comes on a debit card every month, and you can withdraw the cash from an ATM. You can also use this card like a regular debit card to spend on anything you choose.

Government housing: While this exists, I wouldn't depend on government housing as wait lists are long, especially in recent years. Plus, the low-income threshold will keep you trapped in a low-income bracket. If you make too much money, you will lose your housing. You don't want or need any reasons to limit your future income potential.

City welfare: This is highly dependent on the state and area you live in. But your city may have resources to help you with temporary housing. Look up local laws for your area. A low to non-existent income and no safe place to live could qualify you for these services.

In the state of New Hampshire, for example, the town is required to place you somewhere if you show up to the city welfare office or a police station. Usually, it's in a hotel. Sometimes they'll refer you to apartments. They will pay your rent until you can make enough money to support yourself. <u>But you have to know the law and your rights.</u> Otherwise, they may try to jerk you around, such as telling you to go to another town so it doesn't come out of their own town fund.

Is it a good idea to ask friends and family for money?

Asking for money and owing money can ruin personal relationships and can also make you someone's bitch. That's because some people will think they can tell you what to do. So make sure you use discretion in who you ask. You also want to make sure this doesn't get back to your partner. *Just asking for this favor carries a high level of trust, even if the person you are asking says no.*

Although I normally wouldn't recommend this, desperate times call for desperate measures. If you have a trusted, generous, and supportive person in mind, this may work for you. You can also offer to pay them back. This way it's a loan, not a dent in their tight budget.

> <u>Note:</u> If this family member or friend tries to pressure or guilt trip you into returning to your partner—run! This person doesn't have empathy or your best interests in mind. Being around their influence may make you return to your partner. Find another option and don't ask this person for help. Get away from them quickly.

Story time:

Wendy's husband asked for a divorce. He constantly blamed her for his failures at work, and she was feeling worse than ever. After she called him out for this, he said he was done trying to work things out.

So Wendy took all her stuff and moved in with her aunt. As a recent college graduate, she didn't have much real-world job experience. She thought it was okay to not find a job right away, because her wealthy father could cover living expenses. He did give her money. But each time she spoke to him or asked him for anything, he berated her. He shamed her for "failing" in her marriage, not finding a job using her degree, being an embarrassment to the family, and any other life choices he deemed stupid.

Her father also made nasty comments about her to her aunt. This caused her aunt to threaten to kick her out and call her a burden.

Wendy's entire housing and money situation are at the whims of her family, especially her father, and she pays a steep price for it.

<u>The biggest problem is, she doesn't even see it as a major problem.</u> She tells me this is just how her family is and makes excuses for them. But because it's so bad staying with her family, she's considering going back to her abusive husband—as if those are her only two choices.

She doesn't see her third choice: Becoming financially independent and able to control her own life—giving her the freedom to walk away from people who mistreat her.

<u>Credit cards and personal loans—do you qualify for interest-free or low-interest money?</u>

Is it possible to borrow money for free and not accumulate any interest for over a year? If you have good credit, you may be in luck.

You can put expenses on credit cards or take personal loans if you don't have money right now and need to leave very quickly. But if you do it the usual way, the interest rates on these cards are very high. So instead you can look into personal loans, which have better interest rates. But you need to apply, and it's not guaranteed if you don't have a great credit score or income. Often they want even more financial proof, including what you plan to use the money for. It can't hurt to go ask your local, trusted banker for details.

I only recommend these options if you are *very* careful about money and spending. You don't want to end up in debt, paying off high-interest rates, or ultimately filing for bankruptcy.

> **You can use a credit card to your benefit, without paying *any* interest rates. But you need to be completely sure you can pay it off when the introductory period ends—typically after 12 to 18 months.**

Otherwise, you'll end up paying a *lot* of interest. This can help whip your butt into shape and motivate you to get a job to pay it off.

This will only work if you have good discipline with money. You don't want to get stuck paying off several thousand dollars after the one-year introductory period. Some people treat a credit card as if it's Monopoly money and end up spending much more than necessary. This is how people get into debt.

*Pro tip: They will ask for your income. If you apply now, you can include his income. Do not give his name or phone number, or they may try to contact him to verify your income, but they are not strict about this at all. If you don't answer the phone or send proof, they will just give you the card if you have good credit. After getting suddenly kicked out of Michael's, I didn't have a steady job yet. So I put my **expected** yearly income in the box. Guess what? By the time the year was over, I was making more than what I originally told them.*

<u>Note:</u> If you don't have a high enough credit score, credit cards with a o percent introductory interest rate and personal loans may not be available to you.

Check your credit score for free.

> **If you don't know your credit score, annualcreditreport.com is mandated by the US government to provide you at least one free credit report per year. Creditkarma.com is another free service that tracks your credit score and suggests credit cards based on your history.**

You might be pleasantly surprised to have a higher score than you thought, or see what you can do to repair or boost your credit. Even if you never had your own credit card, but were an authorized user on his account, it may have raised your credit score.

<u>You don't want to go to payday loans or loan sharks.</u> They charge a very high interest rate and prey on low-income people who are trapped in the debt cycle. Borrowing and paying high-interest rates just isn't worth it. You are a clever planner—not the type of person who needs this last resort.

Note: Make sure you write a different address on the credit card application and it doesn't get mailed to his house!

Story time:

After leaving Michael, I didn't have a steady job yet and didn't want to deplete my meager savings account. Vince did not give me a credit card or pay any bills like Michael had. So instead, I got a credit card that had a 0 percent introductory interest rate for 14 months, as long as I paid the minimum each month. The minimum was typically $25–35. I racked up several thousand dollars in living expenses. I charged everything I could to this card, including clothing, train fare, car insurance, food, and other living expenses.

Even after I got a decent job, then worked my way into a full-time, good-paying income, I only paid the minimum each month. I put the rest in my savings account just in case. I paid back the full amount due after 14 months and never paid any interest on the card.

This card saved my life in many ways. It enabled me to get back onto my feet and spend money to live my life, while not worrying about accumulating interest. It also served as a countdown timer to get a good job. I promised myself to find a good-paying job to pay the card off before the introductory period ended. The added time limit pressure helped me accomplish getting a job faster.

Let's evaluate your finances

Now that you know how much money you currently have from budgeting secretly and how much you can potentially get from the various methods listed in the section above, fill in these blanks with some number estimates to help you plan.

Moving Expenses

Moving costs depend on where you are moving. You'll need to consider the cost of living in that city, the distance you'll need to move, and if you need to rent a moving van or movers to help you.

How many boxes or containers will you need?	
How many boxes and containers do you already have?	
Names of local restaurants, grocery stores, or liquor stores where you can get free cardboard boxes	
How much will you need to spend on buying boxes?	_____ of boxes x _____ price Total = $
Do you need to hire a moving company or people to help you move big items and furniture?	Hire friends Hire family Hire company
Cost of labor for moving	$_____ per hour x _____ people Total = $
How many trips will it take to move everything?	
What will your gas costs be?	_____(amount to fill up) x_____ (# of times need to fill up) Total = $
Estimated total cost to move	Total = $

Housing Costs

If you're moving in with a friend or family member and don't need to pay rent, skip this section.

Move-in deposit	Total = $
Cost of rent at your new place	$_____ per month x 3 Total = $
Electricity, gas, internet, other utilities	$_____ per month x 3 Total = $
Estimated total housing costs for 3 months	**Total =$**

Other Necessities

If you keep this limited to necessary purchases, these numbers should be low. You want to keep your costs down until you find a stable income. So you likely won't need new clothes for a while, as long as you have a week's worth of outfits to wear. Also, keep in mind that you can obtain free food from food pantries and churches.

Food	_____ / per month x 3 = _____ Total = $
Clothes	_____ / per month x 3 = _____ Total = $
Transportation	_____ / per month x 3 = _____ Total = $
Medication	_____ / per month x 3 = _____ Total = $
Recurring expenses (car payments, insurance, student loan, debt payments, subscription services)	_____ / per month x 3 = _____ Total = $
Cell phone bill	_____ / per month x 3 = _____ Total = $
Total necessities for three months	**Total =$**

Ways to cut down on expenses

How much can you cut down on? Do you need to keep all of your recurring expenses or can you cut back on some?

Cell phone: You can switch to a cheaper cell phone company. If you use a cell phone company like AT&T that charges $60+ a month, consider checking out a cheaper company like Cricket. They cost $30 per month for unlimited minutes, text, and data. And they use AT&T's cell phone towers.

Loans: As far as student loans and debt repayments go, are you paying the minimum? If not, you can lower your payments to the minimum and save the extra cash. Another option is to consolidate your loans. You can research the details online and call them directly to negotiate lower payments based on your income situation. If this pans out, you could be paying hundreds less per month that you can put toward your new living space now. Consolidating loans can help save money in the long run too.

Subscriptions: How about smaller items like subscription services? Do you really need to pay $14.99 every month to access extra news stories on your iPhone? If you have any phone apps that charge a monthly subscription fee, can you find similar phone apps that charge once instead of monthly? You can save a lot of money over time if you cut out $5 every month to use each app.

Are you still getting your money's worth from your Kindle Unlimited subscription right now, even though you're busy planning to move? Do you really need cable TV, Netflix, *and* Hulu? How often do you really use all these services?

Do you subscribe to a monthly box of surprise snacks, clothing, or dog toys?

Putting a temporary hold on your deliveries would save you money and mean accumulating less stuff.

If you do need the subscriptions, could you share some accounts with a friend or family member? For example, you can get one subscription to Sling TV and use it on up to three TVs at a time. This is a cable TV replacement subscription service. So three single people can split a $30 per month service and get most major channels, instead of paying $100+ each for cable—even if they live in different households. For YouTube Premium, it only costs a few more dollars per month to split it with five people than it would for an individual subscription.

Convenience spending: Do you buy a $7 mocha latte every morning at the coffee shop? Yes, I know it's not a lot. But it adds up. Try making your own coffee at home instead for now.

If all these little costs seem insignificant, you're right. Individually, they are. But once you cut down on several of these expenses, you'll start to see a real difference in your monthly statements. Just think of these savings as your "moving expenses" fund. You can always reactivate all your subscriptions later once your housing situation stabilizes.

Total you can cut back on	$
Adjusted necessities total for three months	_____ (total necessities) - _____ (total you can cut back on) **Total =$**

<u>Your Spending Money</u>

Total money needed (add up totals from previous charts)	$
Current available money	$
Money from a family member, church, or other fund? If so, how much?	$
How much do you still need	_____ (total needed) - _____ (total you already have, including church fund and loan from family) $
How much can you make in a month (either from your job or by taking on side hustles to get money)	$
How many months will it take you to save it all	_____ (total needed) / _____ (monthly income)

Even if you have no money now, the ideas listed in "budgeting secretly" and "getting more funds" should give you a good place to start. Once you've acquired your three months of future living expenses, you are ready to take action!

Chapter 3 review

<u>Budgeting secretly</u>

• If he knows the amount of money you have, he'll think he has the upper hand. He'll know *when* you're likely to run out of money without outside funds and try to butter you up to come back.

• If you are married or common law married, don't expect money yet. Courts can take a long time to divvy out the money and assets, and he can drag it out.

• Do you have a personal savings account, or does he have access to it? You need your own secret bank account where you can transfer the bulk of your money. Do not have any bank information sent to the house or stored there.

The many ways to get more funds

• You want to procure moving costs plus three months of living expenses.

• Don't use making money as an excuse to delay leaving for too long.

• You can find many different ways to get money to leave; some of them are better than others.

• Different avenues to obtain money: get a job that pays in cash, sell your services, sell stuff you don't need, save cash your partner gives you, request more cash back than needed on debit card purchases, use local resources and programs, reach out to friends and family, use a o percent introductory interest rate credit card or low-interest personal loans.

• Check out annualcreditreport.com or creditkarma.com to check your credit score for free.

Let's evaluate your finances

• Fill in the worksheet to help estimate your costs for moving, housing, and other necessities, along with how much money you'll need to fund it.

• Keep this list somewhere he won't find it!

• Cut costs by changing cell phone carriers and consolidating student loan payments.

• Think about expenses that aren't necessary. This includes entertainment subscriptions and convenience purchases you can do without or make at home—either downgrade or cut them out for now. This will go toward your moving fund.

• If he's paying for them, just be prepared to cancel your subscriptions and live cheaply for a while, once you leave.

CHAPTER 4

Setting Up Your Own Accounts and Protecting Yourself

S HARED ACCOUNTS? GET YOUR own, and don't tell him!

If you never combined your finances, phone plans, insurance plans, or any other contracts and legal matters with him, congrats! This step will be much easier for you.

If you are married or share accounts for any reason, this chapter will be more important for you. You may find it difficult to protect yourself if you only have shared accounts or he has access to your accounts.

> *But with the advice in this chapter, you will be able to release his grip on you, disentangle yourself, and not have to worry about the repercussions of taking what is yours and disappearing.*

And you'll never have to answer to him again.

Your own, separate accounts represent your freedom—and he knows it. He knows he can't just cancel your access when you've "misbehaved." He can't pull this card to punish and control you. So he will fight it if he finds out you are trying to be financially and mentally independent.

> <u>Hint:</u> Don't tell him! Don't confess when he pulls his usual questioning tactics on you.

How to handle your shared accounts

<u>Joint or shared credit cards</u>

Do you have the same credit card account? If he is the breadwinner, he probably added you as an "authorized user." An added authorized user is different than a joint credit card. It is more akin to adding a minor to use his account. He can see everything you spend money on and your day-to-day activities, but you can't see his.

Being an authorized user is both good and bad. This is good because he is legally responsible for paying the balance, while you have no legal responsibility to pay. He applied for the card and agreed to the user agreement; you didn't. When you leave, you don't have to worry about creditors coming after you. But his payments, non-payments, and canceling your name on the card can affect your credit score. The downside is he can cancel your card at any time without your consent.

If he cancels your card, all your subscriptions, orders, and travel plans will be canceled too. What if you are out when he does this and he suddenly says you can't come back home? What do you do? If you only have that card with you, you are basically screwed.

This is why you must get your own cards and bank account. That way no one can control you or your money.

Don't leave yourself vulnerable to the whims of an unstable or controlling partner. I'm not saying don't spend his money if he is paying the bills still. Spend that money while you can. After all, you are earning it by putting up with his daily bullshit.

But definitely keep your personal backup credit or debit card. Use it for purchases you don't want him to see. And <u>always</u> keep it in a safe place outside your shared home, in case he decides to shut your shared card off. Reference the section later in this chapter for instructions on how to set up your own personal credit card.

<u>Story time:</u>

Michael's temper got so bad that I needed a mental break from him. I left home for two days to stay with a friend. When I was headed to an event the next day, the credit card Michael gave me on our shared account suddenly stopped working. When I called Michael to ask about the card, he started cursing and yelling at me. He said with a tone of victory, "Yes, I canceled your credit card."

This was his revenge for my spending the night elsewhere. So there I was, stranded in the middle of New York City on a Saturday afternoon. All the banks had just closed for the weekend, and I had no subway fare or food money. I tried reaching out to him for help as I told him I didn't have any other credit cards or money with me. But he just said, "Don't come back here.'

Luckily, my friend spotted me some money. And double luckily, I owned a personal Amex card—but I'd left it at home. Amex offered a free two-day delivery on a replacement card. At first, they said it would take a week, but they expedited it when I said it was an emergency. I called customer service, and they were able to ship a new card to my friend's address.

Shared bank accounts

You may have a job and already directly deposit your paychecks into a shared account. Whether he forced you to do this or not, it may be too much of a red flag to suddenly change anything right now. So continue depositing the money there, and then get your share of the money out immediately after you move out. It needs to be before he finds out you left, so he doesn't block your access or withdraw the money.

> **If you decide to withdraw some money early or tell HR to divert some of your paycheck into a different account, have a good excuse—***but only if he asks. He might not even notice or care.***

Some good examples include:

• I'm letting my sister borrow it.

• I need to pay back a large chunk of my college loan to reduce the interest rate.

• I need to buy a new car or parts for my car.

• I had to buy a gift for my brother.

• I've decided to donate part of my paycheck to a charity every month.

• I've decided to take a bigger tax deduction.

When you tell him the reason, make sure it is believable, whether it is true or not. If he asks for proof or paperwork for any paycheck changes, say that you will ask HR for a copy. *Never get frazzled.*

Pro tip: If you get a bigger paycheck, a raise, or work overtime, tell HR to divert this "extra" money into your other account.

<u>If you feel bad about lying about what you're doing with your own money, ask yourself why you have to explain what you're doing with your money at all.</u>

Think about all the stupid things he spends money on and never justifies it to you. You probably don't even know the half of it!

Remember, you are in a code red emergency situation. You need and deserve your money.

> *He'd feel no guilt using money for any of his own needs or whims. And he'd feel no need to explain his actions or reasoning to you.*

With that said, don't over-explain; otherwise, you'll open yourself up to more questions and more suspicion. He may say something disparaging about how you don't need to spend the money. Just ignore him. If he tries to start an argument, don't get into it with him. <u>Don't fall for his line of questioning when he attempts to get you into confession mode.</u>

When it's time to go, take whatever amount from this shared account that you deem fair. <u>Be sure to withdraw the cash instead of doing a transfer.</u> That way he can't trace it to your new account or try to recall the money later.

If you have a separate bank account but you let him use it or he knows the routing number for any reason, you're going to need to cancel that account. If you go to the bank and tell them your account number has been compromised, they will know how to set up a new account correctly.

Story time:

Lisa and Josh seemed like the perfect couple. Before they left New York for Josh's job, I actually deemed them "my favorite couple." But once she followed him out of state, away from all her friends and family, everything changed. He convinced her to get a joint bank account with him. And even though he made five times the amount she did, he required that they contribute the same amount to the joint account.

He went line by line over every transaction from her debit card statement and scrutinized every little purchase. He would ask her what she bought at Walgreens for $3.99 on Tuesday, or why she went to that part of town that day. Yet he never justified any of his spendings.

Luckily, she was able to take most of her share out before she left town. She later told me she felt bad taking anything at all. Of course, Josh called and screamed at her that it's not her money, and she stole from him. Good thing she took it then because he changed all the account information and took her name off the next day.

> *Just ignore his guilt trips. He will say what is fair and favorable to himself only, not the reality.*

Leases and co-signing

If you have a shared rental lease and you leave him, there is a small chance he could stop paying. In this case, the creditors could come after both of you, and he won't care as long as you are going down with him.

If your name is on any leases, count down the days until the lease expires. If you don't want to wait that long, ask, "What would happen if you stop paying it? Does he have the money to pay for it himself? And if not, do you care?"

It could be a hit on your credit score if he decides not to pay it himself. But it may be worth it. Luckily, it won't affect the roof over your head, since you'll be living in a new place anyway.

> *Pro tip: If you have a joint lease that you suspect he won't pay, apply for credit cards before your credit score gets dinged!*

Get independent: Set up your own accounts

No credit? No bank accounts yet? No problem. *It's time to start now.*

Establishing your own accounts is so important because it represents your independence.

The reason he monitors or stops you from getting your own accounts is this helps him retain control over you.

If you don't have good credit or much money yet, it's okay. Everyone starts somewhere.

Set up a private mailbox

You're going to want to set up your own mailbox. Ideally, you'll use UPS or a mailbox with another private company, such as Postal Center USA, or a remote mailbox option, such as Traveling Mailbox, Anytime Mailbox, iPostal1, and Post Scan Mail. These remote ones have an added bonus of scanning your mail so you can see it online without physically checking your mailbox.

> **But all these companies will give you a real street address as your mailbox so people can't tell it's just a mailbox when looking at it.**

They will think it's your actual residence, which is important for several reasons:

• Doesn't leave a paper trail (remote mailbox)

• Gives you privacy since it isn't your home address

• Makes it harder for people to find you as it leads them to your mailbox, not your house (background searches will also point to the mailbox)

• Doesn't let anyone else access your mail

• Safer as a single woman, especially if you have an angry ex trying to find you

• Provides convenience if you move again soon or don't have your living situation set up yet

> **You'll want to list this as your address from now on: on your driver's license, resume, job applications, billing statements, and any other official documents. People who read it can't tell it's not a residential address, unless they're familiar with that exact address.**

They typically offer 3-, 6-, or 12-month plans. Longer plans are typically less per month, but you must pay for it all at once. For a 6-month plan, it's $70+, depending on the area you live in, which is a little over $11 per month. A small price to pay for your peace of mind and privacy.

A "PO Box" doesn't offer the same benefits. It refers to the official US Postal Service mailboxes at a US Post office location. Because it says "PO Box" as part of the address, people can tell it isn't a residential address and you won't be able to use this on all official documents, such as background checks. The post office also won't accept deliveries from other mail services, such as UPS, FedEx, or Amazon delivery drivers.

When to set up mail forwarding: While you can set up this private mailbox while you're still living with him, don't set up mail forwarding with USPS until you move out. A postcard is delivered to the new and old address, informing you that mail forwarding was set up. So he will find out. Plus, it will look suspicious if you stop receiving any mail there now.

Budget option: If you have a tight budget right now, ask a trusted friend or family member if you can send some mail there. Be sure it's someone you can trust not to open your mail that may contain sensitive personal information and won't gossip about it to others. Start changing your address for your bank statements and other important mail now.

Get your savings account and government ID

A savings account is pretty easy to get and often free. In America, all you need is to walk into a bank with two forms of a government-issued ID and a minimum deposit. This can be in the form of cash, a check, or a money order. Nowadays, many banks allow you to easily open an account online; all you need is to include a photo of your ID.

Go local: You're going to want a bank or credit union with a local branch. That way if you don't have your ATM or debit card with you, you can still go in person to get money out of your account. If you already have another bank located in a different city, open a new account in a local bank or credit union. This way you have access to some money locally.

Use a bank or credit union he doesn't use: Open a savings account at a bank or credit union that he doesn't use. This way you won't ever run into him there and no nosey tellers will be able to blow your cover, reducing the chances he'll find out about your account.

Paperless statements: Sign up for paperless statements only. This ensures the statements are sent electronically via email, not the mail. That way there's no paper evidence of your account going to the house that he can snoop around and open or question you about. This is something you can do *today*.

Create a new email address: This goes without saying, but make sure he doesn't have access to the email account you use either. Don't use an email address that you're always automatically signed in to on a shared home computer. If he knows about all your existing email addresses, create a new account that you only use on devices and internet connections he can't monitor. You can use a work or school email address, but it's better to create a new, free one.

Driver's license and ID: Ideally, you have two forms of ID, including a driver's license. If you don't, fix this right away. This restricts your ability to leave and be independent. Replacing a lost social security card, passport, or birth certificate can be done completely online in most cases. Get this mailed to a different address if possible, so he can't intercept your vital documents.

Citizenship, legal immigration status, and rights: You may think you don't have legal status in a country, even if you've been there for a very long time. But there are programs to help. Get legal advice immediately. You can often get a free consultation from a lawyer specializing in immigration law. Just search for immigration law school programs online and contact them. Often, law students set up appointments to give free legal advice under supervision from their law professors. And they do a thorough job because it is part of their grade. You can also check out the legal aid in your town, where many lawyers volunteer to give out free advice as a requirement to keep their law license. There is also legalshield.com—they will answer any legal questions for your specific state and situation for a small monthly fee.

Story time:

Gwen had been working and living in the US and met Will in her early 20s. Once 9/11 happened, it became very hard for her to renew her driver's license because ID requirements tightened. Even though she had been married to Will for over 20 years, he wouldn't hire an immigration lawyer or help her apply for US citizenship.

Everyone assumes she's legal because she is white and has a cute New Zealand accent. But she can no longer drive or legally work in the US and fears getting deported. The narrative that Will spun strips her of basic adult rights. No wonder she doesn't feel comfortable standing up for herself and living alone!

Since she can't renew her ID, she hasn't worked or earned her own money in years and can't get her own bank account. She believes she has nowhere to go if she leaves Will and feels stuck. Even when I told her she would get a nice alimony check if she divorced, his brainwashing that she has no rights prevailed. She says she won't get anything because she's "not supposed to be here."

Believing his story took her power away, and as a result, she couldn't leave him. You need to know this isn't true. Yes, you have a bigger obstacle to face, but you can find ways to leave even if you aren't a legal citizen.

Get a credit card (or debit card)

Earlier in this chapter, I covered how important it is to get your own credit card, instead of relying on a shared credit card.

If you don't have a strong credit score, that's okay. There are special credit cards for newbies. See your local bank to speak to a banker about what they can offer you specifically. You can also search online for "credit cards for people with no credit."

> <u>Note:</u> Look up your credit score for free on annualcreditreport.com or creditkarma.com.

Credit card perks: Credit cards come with some perks, such as earning points toward purchases or cash back. But it's only worth it as long as you pay them off every month. If you're not disciplined enough to pay it off monthly, you could end up paying over 25 percent in interest, not to mention having ruined credit and debt.

Debit cards: So if you don't have a high credit score or don't feel like you have the discipline to have a credit card, don't worry. You can get a debit card, which provides many of the same conveniences as a credit card. But the debit card takes the money directly out of your checking account for each transaction instead of billing you every month. So you'll need the money in your bank account *before* you spend it. It's good because you don't have to worry about late payments, as long as you carry a high enough balance and don't spend more than is in your account!

> Note: You can typically get a debit card with any checking
> account. If you don't have one already, ask your banker how
> you can get a debit card linked to your checking account.

Debit card VS ATM card: You'll know the difference between a debit card and ATM card, because a debit card has a Visa or Mastercard logo. You can use a debit card anywhere Visa or Mastercard is accepted, while you can only use an ATM card to withdraw money from an ATM.

Credit and debit cards are great because you can order what you need online or over the phone with it, plus you can have recurring subscriptions and bills charged directly to it every month. You can also carry less cash with you, and don't have to worry about having enough money with you for big purchases.

Keep your own debit or credit card hidden outside the house in case your move-out is forced earlier than usual. Keep it somewhere he won't find it.

<u>Note:</u> "The many ways to get more funds" section of chapter 3 explains how you can use a 0 percent introductory interest rate credit card as an interest-free loan.

Cell phone plan options

As discussed earlier, you want your own cell phone plan and you may want to secure this before you leave, so you can use your cell phone to discreetly make plans.

No-contract monthly cell phone plans: With the advent of month-to-month plans, there's no need to sign yearly contracts anymore. This also means they are more accessible to everyone and you don't need any credit history. Plans are also super cheap, with some unlimited ones starting at $30 per month with no activation fees. They sell these at stores like Best Buy, Target, and Walmart. If you search online for Cricket, Boost Mobile, and similar competitors, you can probably find even better deals—like free phones and no activation fees.

Cell phone cards by the minute as a backup: An alternative is to buy cell phone minutes, instead of a monthly plan. This is best if you want a backup emergency cell phone just in case, but you don't plan to use it much now. You can pair this cell phone minutes card with an old cell phone you don't use anymore. You need to keep this phone hidden outside the house.

Budget option: In a bind, you can always ask your parents or trusted family member to get on their plan for a while. You don't need to explain why if you don't want to. Just tell them they would be doing you a temporary favor.

> Note: See more reasons on why a phone plan is so important in the "what to be aware of as you plan" section in chapter 2. It covers backup phones, privacy issues, and how he can hold your phone hostage if he ever gets angry with you.

Story time:

During my twenties, it used to be super expensive to get your own phone contract. So I stayed on my parents' family plan.

Michael insisted on adding me to his cell phone plan, but I didn't feel comfortable. Good thing, because when he shut my credit card off, chances are the cell phone would've been next.

Even though I didn't have my account number, I was able to order a replacement Amex card right away because I called from my phone number on record with Amex. This enabled them to verify my identity and information very quickly. They said this would have complicated the process if I'd called from a phone number that wasn't linked to my account. Good thing Michael didn't have the authority to cancel my phone plan!

Safety precautions and considerations

You need to think about your safety. He may act cool for now and like he doesn't care. But what will happen when he knows you're gone and not coming back? You haven't done it yet, so you haven't seen the worst of him.

According to the National Coalition against Domestic Violence, the most dangerous time for a woman in an abusive relationship is right after she leaves. Either threats of separation or actual separations were most often the precipitating events leading to men killing their wives. In 20 percent of cases, homicide victims were not the domestic violence victims themselves, but people who intervened. This includes family, friends, neighbors, bystanders, and law enforcement. [1]

Pro tip: The crazier or more possessive he is, the further away you should move, and the more security you should consider.

> **If he has ever shown physical aggression toward you or others in the past, it will only get worse, especially when he realizes he lost you. If he grew up in a household where he regularly saw physical altercations, he will also feel like this is a natural way of handling things.**

Even if you don't fear him and he ends up not chasing you down, it's a smart idea to protect yourself as a single woman.

Choose a safe living arrangement

Your ideal living arrangement will be around other people. This could mean with roommates, family, or at least in civilization and close to other houses. You don't want to live alone out in the woods.

It's also mentally unhealthy because you may get lonely and miss his company.

When you don't have anyone else, like roommates or family nearby, it'll be easier for him to sweet talk his way back to you.

Another reason you want to live with others is due to physical safety. There is safety in numbers—from unwanted guests, including him. If he drives up and can get to you with no witnesses, it's easy. He doesn't have to worry so much about his reputation or going to jail for harassing, hurting, or kidnapping you. Or vandalizing your property.

See the "types of housing" section in chapter 2 for more specific ideas about living quarters.

Home security: cameras and lights

If you don't live in an apartment complex that already has good security, I'd recommend getting some. Living in a doorman building or a gated community helps, but isn't foolproof.

There are many budget-friendly options as well as more expensive high-tech ones. You don't have to hire a professional security company to install or monitor your system. You can use these budget-friendly ideas to do it yourself. Most of these just include a one-time upfront cost of the equipment. I've listed some options below to get you started. But if you do your own research, you will find tons more.

Motion-detection lights: These are good and cheap. They even have solar-powered lights now so you don't have to have a complex electrical system to connect. And you don't have to worry about changing the batteries. You can put these by all the doors and driveway. And you can put them by the windows, too, especially if they're on the first floor.

These motion-detection lights make it so you can see if someone is outside. It also scares away potential intruders. They know if the light comes on, they just activated something, and you might see them.

Motion-detection cameras: These are also great—especially if you are good with smartphones or computers or have a friend who is and can help you. You can set them up so they start recording if there's motion. There are both indoor and outdoor cameras available.

Doorbell cameras: This is a camera-based doorbell at your front door. It can be good if you aren't home a lot, or don't want people to know when you aren't home. If you don't have a garage and your car is gone, you can't really hide that. You can speak through the speaker on the door as if you are actually home, even though you're just answering through your smartphone. You might be across town, or out of state. But it sounds like you are right there!

A few brands to consider:

Blink ($79+): They offer indoor and outdoor cameras with a two-way talk system, infrared night vision, local storage, and free cloud storage, and the ability to view remotely. There is no monthly subscription and an unlimited amount of cameras can be added.

Ring ($60-$250): They offer doorbells, indoor and outdoor cameras, two-way talk and listening, loud alarm, a camera-floodlight combination that is motion activated that can scare away potential intruders and make you feel safe, and the ability to view remotely. Everything is connected and can be viewed in an app. Cloud storage plans are cheap.

<u>Wyze Cam v3 ($20–$30):</u> This is a budget-friendly option that still works well. It requires double authentication, which prevents hackers from accessing your video stream. You can use it indoors or outdoors, and it has color night vision. It includes a free 14-day rolling cloud storage and can also store videos on your hard drive. There is a pro option, which charges a small fee each month.

<u>Zmodo ($29– $99):</u> They offer inexpensive indoor, outdoor, and doorbell cameras. They offer night vision and motion alerts. If you want more than 12 hours of storage, it costs extra for cloud storage.

<u>Story time:</u>

I had a landlord who put motion-activated lights and cameras near the front and back entrances of the house, as well as one further in the backyard. That way she could see if anyone was trespassing and know ahead of time when a guest pulled into the driveway.

She was older but figured out how to set it up and connect it to her smartphone. That way even if she was away or in a different part of her house, she could watch the cameras. She could also see if motion activated the camera the night before and review the recorded video footage. This made her feel more secure as a single woman living alone.

<u>Self-defense weapons and options</u>

When it comes to protecting your life as a single woman, whether it's from your ex or muggers, I highly recommend choosing at least one of the below options.

> *Just be sure that if you carry a weapon, you are willing to use it
> on someone, even if it means hurting them!* Because they can
> easily take it from you and use it against you.

These are just brief ideas and descriptions. Please research these options more, and find out the legality of possessing and using these in your state.

Pepper Spray: This is cheap and convenient to carry in your purse, and it even works on people who are drunk or angry. You need very minimal training. Just point near their eyes and spray!

Mace: This is similar to pepper spray but is a specific brand name. The chemical substance is different and not as strong as pepper spray. Some people can build up a tolerance to this if they've been sprayed a lot, meaning the more jerky and aggressive the guy is, the more likely he is to be immune to this!

Stun Gun: This delivers a shock to someone. At the least, it will throw off someone's plans if they're not expecting this. These are also cheap and better than nothing.

Taser: This can cost a couple of hundred bucks. But it's much more powerful than any stun gun. It has probes that shoot out up to 15 feet, attaching to the person to shock them. It can immobilize any person, no matter their size, giving you time to get away. People cannot become immune to this.

You have to go through a background check to buy a taser. It is registered in your name, and the new cartridges have info that links the taser to you. Replacement cartridges cost around $20, so it's not cheap for cost per use. And it's not practical to practice with it.

You can only use one cartridge on one person at a time, which poses a problem if you have more than one assailant. Once the cartridge is used, you can still use the end of the taser to physically touch someone and shock them. Despite the expensive price, it's still a good option because it works on every person and causes no permanent damage for most—unless they have a pacemaker.

Knife: A good pocket knife is cheap and compact. A very small blade can make a big impact, especially if an assailant isn't expecting it. They will be shocked, and you'll be able to get away. This requires minimal to no training. Just aim and stab! But can you stab someone and cause them pain, even if they want to hurt you? If you're not confident and you hesitate, an assailant can hurt you with your own knife.

You can have multiple knives. Keep one in your purse, one under your bed, one in your car, etc. These also double as a safety feature to cut a seatbelt loose if you're trapped in a crashed or submerged car, and can't reach the buckle.

Gun: These are expensive and you'll need to pass a background check. They start at around $350 for a decent revolver. You'll also need to target practice, so you get comfortable using the gun. This can be fun. But it also takes time, money, and effort.

Gun laws vary by state. In many states, you'll need a concealed carry permit to carry a gun in your purse. This means spending additional money and taking a test to pass it. Some places, like California and New York City, have extremely strict rules to obtaining permits to carry legally. Most law-abiding citizens in these places don't want to risk breaking the law and having a criminal record.

You'll need to be willing and able to use this if you pull it out. If you hesitate, the assailant can take it away and use it on you instead. You don't want to put yourself in unnecessary danger.

> <u>Note:</u> You can't carry any of these weapons into federal buildings, or most places that have a security checkpoint. Research your local area for the specifics.

Self-defense classes: Sometimes it all comes down to you and them. What do you do if you have no weapon, but they do have one? You'll need to know how to disarm them.

You can take the typical karate, Jiu-Jitsu, or Tae Kwon Do classes.

> **However, a more convenient and quick option is to take a women's self-defense class. Many towns host these, including police departments.**

They typically offer weekend or evening classes so it's not ongoing like the traditional self-defense classes where you achieve different levels or colored belts.

You may feel safer in a women-only environment. And it's fun! You can meet new people and have a good time. Instructors teach you the most vital self-defense moves, including disarming attackers and how to strike them, giving you enough time to flee. You can always take refresher courses on this so you remember all the moves.

I'm not trying to scare you. But it's better to feel safe, secured, and prepared than feel worried and sorry later!

Change up your routine

Most people are very predictable and keep a specific routine. This is what a stalker counts on if he wants to find you. You're going to want to change your routine up after you leave. Do you always go to the same class, gym, running trail, or dog-walking route? How about grocery shopping at the same grocery store—at the same time and day of the week? If so, then you're too easy to find and follow.

If it's possible to switch grocery stores or gyms, it's worth it, especially if it's a place that he frequents or it's near his workplace or house.

You really don't want to tempt fate. Even if you don't think he's violent, you still don't want him showing up unexpectedly. Even if he's just there to make you feel bad or cause a scene in front of everyone, it's not cool. It's easiest to just avoid these locations for a while. <u>You aren't running away. You're being smart.</u> Let him cool down, while you live your life peacefully and privately.

> **It is imperative that you carefully prepare these accounts and safety measures before you leave. The more you detach your identity and resources from his, the more likely your plan will succeed long term.**

Chapter 4 review
Handling your shared accounts

• Don't depend on your shared accounts because he has control over you and can block or cancel your accounts to punish you.

• If you share a credit card, he probably added you as an authorized user, not a joint and equal user, which means he can see all your expenses or cancel your card, but you can't do this to him.

• The primary user is legally responsible for the entire balance; as an authorized user, you aren't responsible for paying off the balance, but the card activity can affect your credit score.

• With shared bank accounts, he can see all your expenses and scrutinize them. The good news is, it will be easy to take the money out of this account that you need.

• If you are on a lease or have cosigned something with him, you can still leave.

• If rent doesn't get paid, they will kick him out. By then you'll already be gone, living somewhere else.

• If rent doesn't get paid, it may ding your credit score. So apply for any car loans or credit cards before this happens!

Get independent: Set up your own accounts

• Get a UPS or other private mailbox to list and use as your address. Use this as your address on record in the future, on resumes, and any other legal paperwork. This keeps your physical home address confidential.

• Select a service that will scan and deliver your mail digitally instead.

• Don't get a PO Box from the US Postal Service, because this doesn't offer all the same benefits.

• Open a savings account at a bank or credit union that he's not a member of.

• Make sure you have appropriate government-issued IDs, such as driver's license, social security card, birth certificate, deeds, and titles to any property.

• Hide these important records in a trusted person's house, locked office drawer, women's locker room gym locker, or safety deposit box.

• Get your own credit card or debit card.

• Select paperless statements so there is no paper evidence of this account in the mail.

• Keep this credit card somewhere outside the house where he won't find out about it.

• Plan to get your own cell phone plan. That way he can't shut it off or monitor you easily as a punishment.

Safety precautions and considerations

• Think about how to protect yourself from your soon-to-be-ex and as a single woman.

• Live with other people if possible. Don't live in the middle of nowhere. This curbs loneliness and is safer.

• Install a security system, either a budget-friendly one or a more expensive high-tech one.

• Motion-detection lights: comes on automatically and can scare possible intruders away.

• Motion-detection cameras: records possible intruders.

• Camera doorbell: allows you to see and speak to people at your front door, even if you aren't home.

• Get some self-protection weapons

• Pepper Spray: cheap, easy to use, legal in most areas.

• Mace: similar to pepper spray, not as strong.

• Stun Gun: vary in strength, quality, and price.

• Taser: expensive but effective and can be used up to 15 feet away.

• Knife: multiple uses but can be taken away and used to attack you.

• Gun: need training, expensive. May need a permit or not be legal in your area.

• Take a self-defense class: Don't need a weapon and will raise your confidence levels.

•. Don't go to the same places at the same times you used to.

• Get a more random routine so you're not easy to find.

National Coalition Against Domestic Violence: Why Victims Stay,
https://ncadv.org/why-do-victims-stay.

Be Smart—the Law Is on Your Side

TRY NOT TO LET your emotions get away from you. <u>Whenever you feel like you need to vent, call up a trusted friend, family member, or therapist.</u> Always think about the long-term and legal ramifications of your actions. Know that the law is on your side, but you need to know the law. Consult a lawyer if there are any legal questions you need to resolve.

Legalities of owning anything jointly

If you are married, have kids, or own anything jointly, it can complicate things. A contract of any kind usually means more paperwork and red tape. But don't let it stop you from leaving, or slow you down too much. The good news is that you likely won't need to pay a lawyer upfront. Most lawyers who practice family law will take your case on a contingency basis. <u>They understand you were a housewife or stay-at-home mother. And if this is the case, you will likely be awarded alimony.</u>

It would soothe a lot of anxiety to speak to at least one lawyer before leaving, even if it's just for a consultation to get some basic questions answered. <u>Many divorce lawyers offer free consultations.</u> You can also join legalshield.com to ask an unlimited amount of questions about your situation, specific to your state laws.

You'll likely find that the beliefs you may hold about not being able to get your fair share of the money or giving up your kids are unfounded. You'll realize your partner fed you lies so you'd be afraid to leave.

> <u>Note:</u> **Please don't say you want very little to no assets just to rush the divorce. In the long run, you will regret it if you don't get what you are entitled to.**

Marriage might work in your favor

A lot of people are ashamed they got married to their toxic spouse because they feel like they made a mistake. Some believe that marriage is forever and take its failure very harshly.

> **But realize you were tricked:** *If you knew how he would treat you before you married him, would you have done it?*

When someone grossly misrepresents themselves, they tricked you into a contract. And you have every right to end the contract.

If people had to stick to being tricked into contracts, we wouldn't have lemon laws for protecting people against being stuck with a lemon car. Nor would we have divorce laws to enable people to leave lemon spouses.

If you regret marrying him, don't. Think logically about this instead of emotionally—you actually have more rights than if you moved in without marrying him.

Focus on moving forward and what you're legally entitled to,
not the mistake.

Your marriage certificate may actually give you legal rights that you wouldn't have had otherwise. If he makes a lot more money than you do, the court can force him to pay alimony. Don't feel bad about making him pay alimony. You deserve it. Let the courts decide what is fair.

Unfortunately, it may take months or longer to see the money. Divorce courts can take a long time. You'll need to be patient. So you're still going to need to rough it in the interim and save up money on your own.

Reminder to secure money: Depending on your situation, you can do what Mary and Lisa did.

Just take half of the money out of the bank account when you are about to leave. Then stash it away.

It's best to take it out in cash instead of transferring it to another account. That way you know it's safe. He can't request the money back from the other bank it's transferred to, cancel the check, or find out about your new account. *If you are going through a divorce, consult your lawyer on this before taking action.*

Story time:

I lived with Michael, and we acted as a married couple for several years. Despite giving up my own career and living as a homemaker, I left empty handed. If I would've just signed the piece of paper he tried to convince me to sign, I would've been able to collect alimony. This would've provided me a cushion so I didn't have to end up living with another narcissist. So it actually would've been in my best financial interest if I would've married him.

The irony is I didn't want to feel trapped, but I was anyway. The trap was ultimately the situation I put myself in, not the piece of paper. I did a wife's duties, but left with none of the benefits.

<u>A note on common law marriage</u>: If you were not legally married, but you lived together for a long time, see if common law marriage exists in your state. Every state is different and some don't recognize it. But if your state does recognize it, and you lived together for the legal minimum length of time, you'd be entitled to half of everything, as if you were legally married. <u>Do your research and consult a lawyer, even if you're not sure.</u> Don't sell yourself short on this!

Your children's best interests and custody

Having children with him definitely makes things more complicated, especially if the kids are young. For one, he can use the kids against you. Even though he may dislike caring for the kids and not want the responsibility, he knows they are important to you, so be aware he could use them as a bribing tool. Also if he doesn't want to pay child support, he may ask for split custody. This also gives him an excuse to communicate with you so there's not a clean break.

> <u>Note:</u> If you just take the kids and leave without a justifiable reason, you could be charged with kidnapping. This could be a felony. Consult with a lawyer who specializes in child

custody battles first. Ask what you need to do in order to leave the *right way*. Each state, length of time, and situation has its unique rules.

If you can prove he's abusive to the kids or abuses you in front of them, or displays other inappropriate behaviors in front of them, do it. Record audio or video, write in your journal, and save the proof. Save multiple backup copies. Do this by taking photos of your entries and backing them up in the cloud. Or saving the typed document to multiple places (see the upcoming section on gathering evidence).

Typically with older kids, they can decide for themselves who they want to stay with. And the court takes that into great consideration.

With this said, you can still leave. Don't let the added complication of kids be the reason you stay. Yes, you have a few more hoops to jump through. But it's totally worth it in the end. After all, it's time to think about what impact this is having on the kids' mental health and development.

Would you want them to follow your example and stay with an abusive spouse? Or to become an abuser themselves? Or be bullied at school because they accept bad treatment as a fact of life and give off victim signals to other kids?

How children are mentally programmed now will follow them throughout their lives.

Story time:

A former coworker named Mary complained about her husband, who cheated on her numerous times and was an emotionally abusive narcissist.

Mary was able to stay at home with her kids while he made a huge salary at a tech company. Even though she referred to him as SD, as in sperm donor, not super dad, she claimed that it was important for both parents to raise a child.

Once her youngest child was old enough to drive himself places, she got a job for the first time in years, withdrew her half of the money, and filed for divorce. Unfortunately, her daughter exhibited similar traits to her father and treated her brother Jay very aggressively. Jay was sweet and had turned into a huge codependent. He was still only a teenager but had already found a very controlling girlfriend, and he gave in to all her demands. Mary didn't like Jay's girlfriend but didn't realize that the reason her son felt comfortable with this behavior was because he watched his own father treat Mary this way. This is the model he had for a relationship and partner. Whereas if she'd left her husband, Jay wouldn't have been exposed to this behavior and may've chosen a healthier, more considerate partner, and her daughter may not have learned aggressive traits.

If you do this the right way and get custody, he will have to pay up.

You should receive both child support and alimony. Then you'll eventually be able to maintain a nice standard of living, without having to compromise. Good things come to those who are patient!

If it makes you feel better to hire a lawyer before you get out, do it. This makes even more sense if your situation is complicated, such as needing to extract your children safely and legally.

<u>Don't give in</u>

Some women will get emotional about this process and then end up giving in to his terms. Once you've made a decision and realize what outcome you want, it's hard not to give in so you can leave. It's understandable, you just want your current situation to go away and move on quickly.

But don't rush the divorce without getting the best terms for you. Or if you signed a prenuptial agreement, don't think that means you can't get anything. And definitely don't let him guilt trip you into thinking you don't deserve anything. And if you have kids, stand up for their rights.

Speak to your lawyer about any of the above concerns. They can help you handle a lot of the ugly legal stuff. And they know their way around the law and how to best help you.

> **Above all, remember you are not alone in this, especially if you are someone who is used to having to do everything yourself.**

Do not hesitate to use your outside resources.

He may also start pressuring you to sign documents. If this is the case, take the documents to a lawyer immediately. If you're still living there, leave if he threatens you and makes you feel unsafe. <u>Just don't sign anything when under pressure!</u>

He is probably used to getting his way. And you giving in to whatever he says. Don't let him run his mind games on you. Let your lawyer handle this. She will probably tell you to stop speaking to him directly.

Finally, you'll get peace and what is fair for you based on facts and the law, instead of what he wants you to believe.

Finding a lawyer

Please consult a lawyer in your state about any pressing questions before you make any rash decisions. It's a good idea to go in with a list of questions, such as timing, how much alimony you may get, etc.

Hire the right female lawyer

Your best bet is hiring a female lawyer, who specializes in representing women. I don't recommend a male lawyer because it's going to be harder for them to empathize with a stay-at-home wife. They may feel they've been screwed over by an ex-wife in this situation and paid a lot of alimony themselves. This will make them biased.

Plus the right female lawyer is more likely to fight harder for you based on principle, if she can empathize with your situation. Directly ask her about the gender ratio of past cases she's represented. Ask her if she's represented many clients in your situation before.

Pay close attention to *how* she answers the questions, not just the words she says.

Observe how comfortable she is taking this case on a contingency basis. This will give you clues as to if she's the right one.

<u>Note:</u> Beware of female lawyers who hate other women and represent more men. Some women also look down on women who don't have to work outside the home. Be aware of these types of female lawyers during your search process.

Remember, you are interviewing her as much as she is interviewing you! You need to feel confident that she is the right one who will fight for your best interests.

How to find her

To find an empathetic female lawyer, ask around for strong referrals and recommendations from agencies or friends who've hired one themselves. Also, check the bar association's website in your state for a list and go to a local law clinic at a law school near you. Once you have someone in mind, do a quick search on the internet to see if she has any reviews.

Feel free to see several different lawyers for free consultations. It's good to have a strong basis of comparison. You want to assess what each lawyer can try to get for you, how much they will charge, and who you like best. Base your choice on your findings, including:

• her knowledge and experience

• personality compatibility

• responsiveness to you

• results of her past cases

• the speed of her typical cases to close

<u>Note:</u> Beware of smooth talkers who make a lot of promises that sound too good to be true. Verify it with facts and evidence that they've been able to achieve these results in the past.

> **Pro tip:** Whenever one spouse consults with a lawyer, the lawyer often won't represent the other spouse. This is because the lawyer now knows too much about the opposing side. Even if they don't take the case, it would be a conflict of interest. This is another reason why it's important to find the right lawyer quickly and discreetly.

Gathering evidence

These are general guidelines for gathering evidence. As a rule of thumb, you want to document the ways that make him a bad, abusive, or unstable husband and/or parent. You want to document how much money, property, resources, investments he makes and has.

> **The best evidence is voice recordings, video, and photographic proof because it's hard to refute.**

When you meet with the lawyer, tell her about all the evidence you have already gathered. It's easiest if you gather this along the way, not in a mad scramble at the end. Your lawyer will be able to give you more guidance on what you need to save and document for your individual situation.

<u>Keep records of the money</u>

Take photos or copies of all records of assets you can find. This includes

• bank statements with balances

• investment statements

• his paycheck stubs

• pension contract or 401k retirement contributions

• property assessments

Most of these records come in the mail, so once you leave, you won't have access to them. To get your own copies, snap a pic with your phone camera when he's not looking.

> **If you don't bring your own copies to court, it'll be easier for him to hide them.**

The different ways to document abuse

If it's physical and there are bruises, cuts, broken bones, then, hopefully, you've been to a doctor. Set any embarrassment aside. Please tell the doctor everything so they can write it down. This creates a record. If there are police reports, this also creates a record you can use.

Even if you don't have outside records, you can take your own photos of your injuries and write detailed journal entries about what happened. Be sure to write the date and time. If you can discreetly take video or audio recordings of altercations, that's even better.

<u>If you never photographed your injuries or saw a doctor about them, you still have options.</u> If you have witnesses who've seen the bruises, they can testify against him. You can also take photos of any broken furniture, lamps, walls, or belongings that he may have damaged in his anger. Save any emails or text messages you may have sent regarding these incidents.

<u>If it's mental or financial abuse, you can also describe these events in your journal.</u> *Give details, receipts, bank statements showing any money or resources he took from you.* If he damages your property or there are holes in the wall from him shoving you, also take photos and write detailed accounts about it in your journal.

<u>Using a secret voice or video recorder may be an option to document his threats or physical intimidation.</u> But in a few states, it's illegal to record something without both parties' consent, so ensure this doesn't apply to you.

How to document cheating

Take photos of receipts showing dinners or gifts he bought for someone else he's seeing on the side. I would say an affair, but it could be a prostitute or one-night stand. Save any text messages, emails, phone records, lewd photos, or anything else that helps prove his cheating.

If you have audio or video recordings of the incident or him confessing to you, keep those. I'm not saying to follow them, but if you have photos of them together, especially in romantic poses, those can serve as evidence too.

If either of you tests positive for sexually transmitted diseases (STDs), save those documents as well.

<u>Collect witness accounts</u>

Get the contact info of any witness who has seen his ugly behavior toward you. Ask them for their numbers before you leave. If they can write and give you a signed statement now, even better. Just know that some may back out if they need to testify in court. Many people are cowards and get scared easily, especially if they are his neighbors and will still need to deal with him.

<u>Keep a detailed journal</u>

Keep a journal on all the ways he has mistreated you, including events that led up to you leaving, whether it is physical, verbal, or financial abuse. That way you aren't blamed for "abandoning the marriage," while he looks like a perfect little prince in court.

Include dates, times, what he said or did to you, and any other details. All this can help you in court.

And it'll also help to serve a dual purpose of reminding you why you left in the first place. If you ever miss him or get an itch to go back, read your journal!

<u>Note about safely keeping your own copies:</u> Give *copies* to your lawyer. But always keep a copy of all evidence too. This is just in case something gets lost or happens to your lawyer. Remember, no one cares more about your case than you do.

<u>Note about keeping evidence discreet:</u> Knowledge of this evidence is on a need-to-know basis! Do not let other people know that you are collecting or possess this evidence. If he finds out, he may become enraged and try to hurt you. Or he may prepare a better defense against you in court. Just stay quiet about it, and you'll be fine. If in doubt, play dumb.

Hardball strategies

Sometimes you have to play hardball and kick him where it hurts to protect yourself.

So, if he's somehow found a way to contact, hassle, or stalk you, you have options to consider.

You can file a restraining order

If he starts popping up in your new life, this can be scary, even if he doesn't say anything directly to you or about your past relationship. If you see him driving by your house or hiding in the bushes, this is even scarier.

But you do run these risks anytime he finds out where you work or live or your schedule. If you don't reply favorably to his phone or online messages, expect him to take more drastic measures. He'll know his pull over you is fading.

> **He knows the same fact that we do—the longer you are outside his sphere of influence, the more likely you won't go back.**

Once you feel the freedom of living without him, his chance of pulling you back into his lair decreases. So he may get desperate.

Be sure to document dates, times, any witnesses, and details of coming into contact with him. Save any voicemails, messages, and times you bump into him. He might be nice at first, but may go off the rails if he loses his cool.

If you feel unsafe, consult a lawyer or ask the police if you can file a restraining order against him.

If they say no, ask what you need to do, and go from there.

Don't be afraid to file police reports

If you find anything missing, vandalized, or any threatening signs, file a police report. You can use this to recover damages through insurance or the court system.

A paper trail is important if this continues, ensuring you have an official record showing his pattern of behavior.

You don't have to press charges and no one has to find out. Don't get caught in trying to decide if you should or shouldn't report it—you always should. You can decide later what you want to do with the report after it's done.

Report him to his job as a last resort

You may feel bad about doing this. But if he won't stop bothering you and you've tried everything else, this may be your last resort.

Police reports are usually not advertised to the public, unless it's an arrest or something major. So you may need to find a way to publicly humiliate him or jeopardize his reputation. Do something that will affect his income or professional career. The best way to do this is to report him to his job or an organization he belongs to where he's respected.

Story time:

After Michael kicked me onto the streets of New York and his anger died down, he realized this move could be detrimental to his career, as I could call his job with one phone call, and his career would likely be over. Michael worked for a religious organization, where he was up for tenure. They cared about their employees' moral character. He'd also lied about his religion in order to get the job and generous salary—which is more dirt I could report him for!

Even when I wouldn't move back in with him, he started paying me a weekly cash allowance as hush money. He continued to pay until I was able to find a job. This was his insurance policy so I wouldn't squeal on him to his boss about how he treated me and reveal his true moral character.

If I would've called his boss, he almost definitely would've lost his job. He was up for tenure, and a couple of people in his department didn't like him. How he treated his partner could've been the tiebreaker for them to get rid of him. The threat of this was enough to make him behave; he temporarily gave me money and stored my stuff. And it wasn't just out of the goodness of his heart.

If he has a job that needs a security clearance or if he is in the military, special rules apply to him. It'll be harder for them to turn a blind eye, and this can make him be demoted or even lose his job if it keeps happening.

Story time:

When my friend Jill was little, she watched her dad beat her mom up frequently. One day her mom had enough. She called the military police. Her father was demoted and had his pay temporarily reduced. This was his only warning. They told him on his next violation, he'd be kicked out of the military. Even though the mental abuse and cheating continued, he never hit her again after this incident.

Don't feel sorry for him if he is hurting you and won't leave you alone.

If you show you are willing to report him, it will hopefully be enough to spook him so he leaves you alone. Be sure you report him after you are safely away from him, because it could easily backfire if he has low self-control. Jill's mom took a huge chance by reporting her spouse she still lived with. It could've turned out much differently.

If you have any legal ties such as marriage, kids, or joint ownership together, gathering your evidence and finding an excellent lawyer is key.

> *It's vital to learn your rights, stick up for what belongs to you, and not believe all the stories he's tried to scare you with.*

Chapter 5 Review

Sitting down with a lawyer for an initial consultation to answer basic questions will make you feel better about moving forward.

Legalities of owning anything jointly

• It can complicate things if you have any legal ties to him. But don't let it stop you. It'll just take a little more planning and preparation.

• Don't see marriage as a bad thing. You have more rights and are entitled to your fair share if you're married.

• If you move in without marrying him and your state doesn't support common law marriage, you are entitled to little or nothing, so research your state to see if they recognize common law marriage. If so, and you've been together for the minimum amount of time, you could be entitled to half of everything as if you were married.

• If you have kids together, consult a lawyer on your rights before you take off with the kids and get a kidnapping charge against you.

• Don't get emotional and give in to his terms.

• Don't rush the divorce and not get what you legally deserve.

• You aren't alone in this. Your lawyer knows the law and will fight for your rights.

• Don't give in to him pressuring you. Just because he says it, doesn't make it true.

Finding a lawyer

• Find a female lawyer who mostly represents women.

• Beware of lawyers who may be bitter about homemakers getting their fair share.

•. Many lawyers will take a case on a contingency basis if they think they can win you money.

• Be sure to ask for recommendations from people who've actually used this lawyer. Take positive and negative reviews into account, based on your needs.

• Don't be shy about seeing several lawyers for free consultations, especially if they are lawyers he may want to hire.

Gathering evidence

• Document any statements regarding bank accounts, assets, and his income.

• Take photos and recordings of any type of abuse, whether it's physical, mental, cheating, etc.

• Give copies to the lawyer and retain your own backup copies—just in case.

Hardball strategies

• You can take legal steps to protect yourself and your privacy. Don't feel bad about taking these! Use them as a last resort if he misbehaves.

• File a restraining order against him if he keeps bothering you. Talk to your lawyer and the police about this.

•. If anything feels off or your stuff gets damaged or starts disappearing, file a police report.

• You don't have to decide whether to press charges now. But the paper trail is there if you need it in the future. It can also be used to file claims for insurance purposes.

• Sometimes people need to be publicly humiliated to stop acting like an asshat, so in that case, report him to his job. If his image or job is important to him, this will show him you are serious. Only do this once you are safely gone.

Next, we'll talk about the mental aspect of leaving, such as how to act and whether to give him a heads up about your plans or not.

CHAPTER 6

Stay Quiet and Keep Your Cool Before You Leave

Y OU MAY WONDER IF you owe him an explanation for leaving or if you should tell him ahead of time. You may even be so upset with him, you want to throw it in his face to punish him.

Deciding to tell him or not

If you feel the need to tell him or just want to throw it in his face, ask, "Is it more important to leave safely and peacefully, or do you want to start an argument and see his reaction?

> **What advantage would you possibly get from telling him? Do you secretly want him to stop you from leaving? Do you want him to apologize and promise to change?"**

You have already given him plenty of chances to change. If you think you haven't, then why are you moving out?

Assuming you do want to get out without any complications, you need to lay low and not stir anything up right now.

This ultimately comes down to how dangerous and toxic you think he could get. Refer to the section "How quickly do you need to leave?" in chapter 2.

<u>I highly recommend not saying anything until after you safely move out.</u>

Story time:

The day before leaving Vince, I told him I was leaving. He didn't have a day job, so he sat around the house a lot of the day. I couldn't sneak out, and I still had a carload of things to move out. So I figured what's the harm?

Since he had been convincing me to get a better-paying job in Washington DC, I told him I went ahead and followed his advice. I thanked him for trying to help me and said my new success was all due to him. The location wasn't accurate, but I didn't want him to find out where I was really moving. Also, he didn't actually want me to move; he said it just to act like he didn't want or need me around.

He remained calm while tears flowed down his face. There was no guilt-tripping me or convincing me to stay. At first, I thought he took this much better than I thought. I breathed a sigh of relief and let my guard down. I told him I was leaving that night, and I was on a tight schedule due to my training starting.

He asked me if he could take me out to eat to celebrate. We usually went to the place of his choice—but he told me to choose any restaurant. I felt excited and relieved. We ended up at one of my favorite restaurants. One he would've normally shunned, due to the healthy menu. We shared a few different dishes. He seemed to love the food. I thought we were having a great time.

But after I came back from the bathroom, he refused to eat any more, even when I put a bite of delicious dessert up to his face. In retrospect, this was a huge red flag. I should've stopped eating too. But since he acted so happy for me, I lowered my defenses.

Walking back to our apartment, I started to lose all energy. I could barely walk all of a sudden and felt like passing out. At this point, all Vince's kindness evaporated and he kept walking quickly, as if I wasn't even there.

Luckily, I was only a few blocks away from the apartment. I called my best friend and told him not to come yet, because I suddenly felt very exhausted. I told him I needed to rest before I moved the rest of the stuff out. He said okay, but reminded me I needed to leave that night. I couldn't miss my arrival time for training; otherwise, I would lose my job offer!

I napped the rest of the evening. I couldn't finish packing. When my friend came to help me, I could barely move or speak coherently. He said I wasn't in my right mind. He had to drive me the entire way to training because I couldn't stay awake, and I felt sick. He later told me that he knew Vince drugged me, but he didn't want me to panic.

If not for my best friend driving me several hours away to training, I would have missed my opportunity to leave. Vince knew this and tried to stop me. Despite all the "values" he preached and how much he acted like I was an inconvenience to him, he drugged me to stop me from leaving! Learn from my naivety and don't take any chances when it comes to securing your future and safety.

~⋖≫

If you decide you want to tell him, don't give much notice. Even if you tell him the day before, he can still try to thwart your plans! Also, give yourself plenty of time to get where you're going. That way if he tries to derail your plans and you miss your deadline, you aren't totally screwed.

Whatever you say, it doesn't have to be fully true. You won't want to say anything at this point to hurt his ego, especially if he's a narcissist or prone to losing his temper.

> *This isn't about lying or the truth—this is about protecting his ego so he doesn't retaliate.*

Keep it vague. Say you got a job offer or are moving to help an ill family member. Try to link it back to something he's suggested to you in the past. *Make him think it was his idea, and you took his suggestion*! <u>Don't say it's because you don't want him anymore.</u>

Expect him to ask questions, but only give him the basic minimum. *If you don't think you can do this and will end up having diarrhea of the mouth and telling him everything—then don't give him any warning.*

> **It's none of his business what you do next. You aren't making joint decisions anymore. You don't need his input. You are trying to separate your life from his—not ask for his permission or get his blessing.**

The last thing you want him to do is to thwart your plans.

Tricks to get you to confess your plans

Be careful, because sneaky people know how to draw out confessions. They use certain tactics to get long-winded explanations and confessions. But *remember—he knows nothing.*

As long as you know you've been vigilant, he doesn't know anything. He definitely doesn't know the dates, times, and places you lined up. He might suspect, but he doesn't know. If he shares his suspicions, this just gives you more insight into his thoughts. It means you're doing something to reveal that something is different about you.

If you can figure out what behavior is tipping him off, then change it so he calms down. Be prepared for him to use any of the tricks mentioned below to get you to confess.

He may use awkward silence as a weapon

When someone is silent, it brings out the codependent in us. Most people are uncomfortable with silence, so they just start spewing free information, showing all their cards, and tipping off their thoughts and plans to the abuser. If you do this, you will regret not keeping your mouth shut. The information you reveal *will* be used against you. This is a typical technique police use when trying to get confessions from suspects.

He may ask questions and suddenly seem concerned about your well-being

He might start asking you what you think about your relationship, if you're happy, or where it's heading. This sudden, feigned concern is to make you feel comfortable enough to confess to him.

> **Don't fall for it and tell him the truth: that you're unhappy, leaving, and there's nothing he can do about it now. What good would this do?**

Instead tell him that everything is okay, the same as always—or whatever it is you would normally say to him before.

He may mirror your language

He may start repeating what you say slowly. He may even mirror your body language and movements. This psychology trick makes us feel understood. It makes us want to further explain ourselves. Don't fall for this!

He may grasp for straws and try to guess

He may start talking about something as if he already knows you did it, even if he has no evidence or only a tiny shred of evidence. This could be based on your nervousness or different behavior lately, a place he thinks you might've been, people he knows you like to speak to, or somewhere he suspects you're moving to. Don't take the bait.

He may ask in many different ways til you confess

When someone wants you to admit to something, they will try to ask you over and over, in many different ways. They are hoping to tire you out or catch you off guard in a moment of weakness.

He may ask when you feel tired

He may ask when you are tired, knowing you aren't as guarded then and may slip up during this time. This includes early in the morning or very late at night. He may watch out for lower mental alertness, such as if you just worked a very long shift.

Stay focused

Don't be suspicious or act differently. Otherwise, he'll catch on that something has changed and will keep digging deeper. You are on the home stretch—almost there! If he tries to trick you, just stay focused and use the tactics below.

Stop yourself when you go into confession mode

Confession mode is something you'll need to recognize to stay out of trouble.

Being in a relationship with someone like this has groomed us to confess. So we often give much more information and details than necessary. Not just in this situation, but in every situation! This is how he keeps tabs on us and controls us.

You need to start noticing when you say too much and practice saying less.

What can you say in a more succinct way without unnecessary details, even when you have nothing to hide?

This will help curb your habit of going into confession mode. It'll also help prepare you to blend into society better and not get taken advantage of by others. This will come in handy when you're out in the real world again, job hunting and meeting new people.

Give default answers to throw him off

If he is acting out or asking you a lot of questions, you are probably giving something away. If in doubt, stay silent, or give him a default answer you would've said before. Think about which default answers still make sense now. Say whatever will throw off any suspicions and calm him down.

To do this, you can subtly let him know you are preoccupied with some other outside issue, which explains why you may be acting differently. *Remember to withhold details.*

Some default answers that may give the illusion that you're preoccupied with an outside issue include:

• Arguing back with him when he criticizes you

• Complaining about the neighbors or your job

• Saying how worried you are about a family member or friend who has had problems in the past

• Giving any other complaint you've said to him in the past

Familiarity will put him at ease, and quell his suspicions. If you can't think of anything to say, nod in agreement with him. Don't expound on any details if he asks open-ended questions to find out more. This may drive him crazy, especially if you've never behaved this way before.

> **Come up with your default answers now and rehearse them, as you never know when you may need them.**

He may confront you at an unexpected time. When you're in the moment, it's so easy to falter. You can read all this and logically understand it now. But when he ambushes you, what will you do then?

It's so easy for all this to go out the window, for you to go back into default mode. This is new, and you've been operating in a totally different way throughout the relationship. Will you panic and not answer fast enough, then revert back to going into confession mode? *Not if you have practiced your answers.*

Don't act too happy

I know you may feel happy and excited about leaving. But don't show this to him, especially if you didn't act that way before. He will probably try to ruin your mood anyway since toxic people don't want to see you happy.

A toxic partner is an insecure partner. An insecure partner picks up on any subtle changes. So he will double down and become more vigilant about watching you.

If he asks you why you're so happy or acting different lately, what will your response be?

> *I recommend telling him some news that has to do with a friend or family member.*

Some examples are:

• a friend getting married

• a relative having a baby or getting a pet

• your brother getting accepted into his dream college.

It's best to make it loosely based on a real event, but it doesn't need to be. If you can't think of something, base it on something you saw on celebrity news. Practice not going into confession mode, and don't tell him details.

> **If he presses you, turn it around on him by asking him if he's happy about it too.**

Whoever asks the questions controls the conversation. You can also walk into another room or change the subject quickly after.

Don't assume he has any knowledge

If he acts like he knows something, he probably doesn't. Toxic partners recognize patterns and changes in patterns. If your patterns changed, it's normal for him to ask more questions. Just don't fall for his open traps. Don't assume he already knows. He wants you to think he knows, that way you "behave" the way he wants you to. But he doesn't know everything.

It's just that you "behave" a certain way to avoid upsetting him. He purposely focuses on what you are doing, your mistakes, and your actions that upset him. He doesn't want to talk about his actions or wrongdoing.

> **While you are focused on not doing anything wrong, he is getting away with whatever he wants.**

If he knows he has you looking over your shoulder because you feel like he's watching you, he knows he is in control. **In reality, he only knows what you tell him or show him.** Whatever you do, do _not_ start confessing!

Stay involved and distract yourself

Try to get involved in extracurricular activities outside the house, even if your extracurricular activity is working or spending more time out of the house, to make your escape plans. It'll keep you busy and your mind occupied. Sometimes if you have too much spare time to think, it can psych you out. Don't overthink or overcomplicate it. Just keep taking action toward your goal.

Plus, an added bonus of staying involved in other activities is that you'll be away from him, which means less of a chance to give off signals that something is different.

Your big day

This is the day of truth. It's everything you've prepared for. By now, you've lined everything up. Ideally, you've moved out most of your stuff that you want to keep or, at least, packed it into boxes. That way, you can move it out quickly, preferably within a few hours.

Safety first

If you have any doubt about your safety or if he'll stop you from taking your stuff out, call the police. Tell them you are moving out. Let them know the date, address, your contact number, and name. Don't be afraid to call them if he shows up early or if you otherwise feel uneasy. They will also usually wait with you while you move stuff out or drive by to check up on you if it's an all-day event. (See the section "Do you need backup on move-out day?" in chapter 2.)

Be ready to move

• Have all your stuff already in boxes and ready to move out quickly. This is less time you have to spend on this. Prioritize your most expensive and prized possessions first, just in case you run out of time. Have those at the top or front of the pile. (See "what to pack" in chapter 2.)

• If you're using a moving truck, have it scheduled. Confirm the appointment.

• Make sure your friends or movers get there at your specified time and you have a van or moving truck ready to load up.

• Make sure your gas tank has plenty of gas.

• Ensure you budgeted enough time and room to bring everything you want to take.

• Double check the place you plan to take your stuff, whether it's a friend's house, your new place, or storage unit. Ensure you have the keys and that it'll be ready for you when you arrive.

• Have dependable friends on standby to make sure you got out okay. They need to hear your voice, even if it's just a quick phone call.

• Post office mail forwarding. You can set this up online with a credit or debit card, for a buck. You can always go in person to the post office if you don't have a card to use. (See "Get independent: Set up your own accounts" in chapter 4.) But make sure it's *after* you are gone. A postcard will arrive in the mail saying your mail is being forwarded, and he will see it. But it won't reveal your new address.

• Optional: disable social media accounts like Facebook. If you don't want to disable your accounts, at least unfriend or block him on there. You don't want him spying on your activities or making stupid comments. Don't do this till you're completely moved out; otherwise, it might tip him off that something changed.

By this point, you've done most of the work and know you are on the home stretch. But you are still not out yet, so it's important to do this last part right and not get careless when you can see the finish line. Stay focused.

⌐<o

Chapter 6 Review

Deciding to tell him or not

• What advantage would you get from telling him? If you want to provoke him or get him back, this isn't the time or way to do it.

• Remember, if you make a serious plan to leave, telling him will likely hamper your plans and make it harder to get out.

• Don't worry, your revenge is leaving. You won't see the fallout. But trust me, there will be one behind closed doors.

• If you decide to tell him, don't give him much notice. Tell him the day of.

• I recommend not telling him anything till you're gone!

Tricks to get you to confess your plans

• Awkward silence as a weapon: this brings out the codependent in us and gets us to confess.

• Asking questions, suddenly seeming concerned about your well-being: he'll try to pull on your heartstrings, to make you feel comfortable and relaxed to the point you confess.

• Mirroring your language: if he repeats the last few words you said, this psychology trick makes us want to further explain ourselves. He may also mimic your body language to put you more at ease.

• Grasping for straws, guessing: He doesn't actually know anything if you've been careful. He just knows you're acting differently. But even if he does know something is up, so what? You don't benefit by admitting to anything.

• Asking in many different ways: he may ask you the same question in many different ways, hoping you will eventually trip up and confess.

• Asking when you feel tired: when we are tired, we aren't as on guard.

• Remember—he knows nothing. There may be something you're doing that's tipping him off that something is different, so figure out what that is and change it. But don't admit anything.

Stay focused

• Don't act differently whatsoever. You don't want to tip him off.

• Stop yourself when you go into confession mode: Practice noticing when you do this, then stop yourself. Say less and don't give any details.

• Give default answers and practice saying them: Think about what you would've normally said in the past. Make it more succinct. If in doubt, stay silent. If you get stuck, nod your head to agree with him. But this may drive him crazier, especially if you've never done this before.

• Don't act too happy: If you start acting differently, he will get insecure and suspicious. Use a story about a friend or relative's good fortune. Something he can't ruin or control. If you can't come up with a story about a friend or relative's good news, use a celebrity story.

• Don't assume he has any knowledge: Turn it around on him by asking what he thinks or knows about the news you just mentioned. In order to keep you in line and "behaving," he acts like he knows more than he actually does. He knows far less than he lets on. If you keep your mouth shut and keep your plans hidden, you are golden. He only knows what you tell him.

• Stay involved and distract yourself: Spend more time outside the house, even if it's just to go to the park or library and plan your move. The more time you spend away from him, the less chance you'll give away that something changed.

Your big day

• Call the police to notify them if you're afraid of a run-in.

• Your remaining stuff should be packed and in boxes.

• Plan for the arrival of your moving truck and any help you'll need.

• Double check that your destination is ready for your arrival.

• Make sure your friends will call to check on you later that day, to ensure you got out.

• *Set up mail forwarding* at the post office or online. But, ensure it's scheduled for after you've already left.

• Temporarily disable social media to keep stalkers, drama, messages, and emotions at a minimum for a while.

CHAPTER 7

After Thoughts and Mind Games

Go no contact if possible

I T'S BEST IF YOU can go no contact and stop talking to him, at least for now. <u>If he's going to have a problem and be upset that you left, block his phone number.</u> This is the best option if you have no further reason to talk to him. You can always reach out in the future once some time has passed, if you change your mind.

When you start to get lonely and remember the good times with him, you may want to reach out to him. *But it's a terrible idea.* This is exactly why you need to surround yourself with good people and roommates during this time. You don't want him to sweet talk you into going back to him—or for him to find you or hurt you.

> **At this point, interacting with him is a waste of your time and mental energy.**

If he keeps bothering you, using different phone numbers to call you, or having his friends and family text and call you, you can change your number.

Story time:

When Lisa left Josh, her fiancé, she knew she never wanted to go back. She was moving back to her hometown, several states away from him. Even though she blocked Josh's number, he would message or call her from other phone numbers. She changed her number a couple of days later so it would stop.

He started messaging her on every social media and email account—even creating new email accounts to contact her. Luckily, they had no mutual friends, so he couldn't use them to spy on her.

Over a year later, he tried again to contact her. He started off nice by congratulating her on her new job and saying happy birthday. But once he had her responding, he slowly dropped the nice guy act. He guilt tripped her for abandoning him, reminding her that their wedding day was coming up. After a few weeks, she realized it had devolved from seemingly innocent to mean.

He blamed her for ruining their engagement and would never see or admit to anything he did wrong in the relationship. Despite his initial kind messages, he would never change. He was making her feel terrible again, so she cut him off once more for the last time.

The grey rock method alternative

If you have kids or any other legal ties together, you may have to keep some contact with him. This is where the grey rock method comes in.

Pretend to be a literal grey rock. What would a grey rock do if it was getting yelled at and a crazy-acting person tried to provoke it? <u>That's right—a rock</u>

would show no reaction.

This method also includes speaking to him as minimally as possible and giving short responses.

> **Don't engage emotionally or react to ludicrous or awful statements about you, and don't be afraid to stop responding.**

If you must speak to him, lead him back to the subject you need to discuss if he gets off track, without showing any emotional reaction. D*on't even acknowledge any rude and inappropriate statements.*

> **He will say things to provoke you and knows how to push your buttons. Don't fall for it or fight with him. That's what he wants.**

Example grey rock responses

Use these examples to guide you:

Example 1) If he says, "You're always like this. Late and making excuses. You blame me for everything as if you're the victim. But it was your fault for being a bad mother."

You respond, "I will be in the driveway at two p.m. to pick the kids up."

Example 2) If he says, "How come you're so rude? Your PMS and mood swings are the reason we had to break up."

Simply respond, "I'll take the evening shift and be there from three–nine p.m."

Example 3) If he says, "You didn't schedule the delivery again?! Just like you neglected the maintenance on the pipes and they ended up bursting and costing us thousands of dollars and unnecessary agony. How did you get through college? How did you survive before meeting me?"

Respond, "The delivery is on Friday from one–two. Meet Mike out back and have the empty canisters ready."

Have you ever heard the quote "Don't get into the mud with the pig because the pig likes it!"? Well, he is the pig. And he likes when you stoop down to his level and engage with him. <u>While he is enjoying it, you are not.</u>

Go through your lawyer if he gets too out of hand. The good news is, if you stick to text messages and emails, it's all on record in case you need to get the court involved. You can save these inappropriate messages as evidence of his behavior. Show your lawyer, because you may be able to use them in court against him (refer to chapter 7).

❧

If he tries to suck you back in

Unless he's the one who chose to end the relationship, take caution. He will probably try to suck you back in. It is vital for his ego that everything ends on his decision and his terms—or he will definitely be back.

If you left him and left any loose ends, like any open communication channels that he knows about, he will try to contact you. Expect this. He may hope you'll trip over yourself to try to apologize. <u>The sooner he can convince you,</u>

the more likely you are to fall back into old patterns and fall under his spell again.

> **The longer you breathe freely and get perspective, his power over you will diminish. He knows this!**

Baiting pattern of a narcissist or verbally abusive partner

Step 1: Blaming and shaming. He'll chastise and shame you for leaving or blame you for whatever "sin" he claims you committed for him to kick you out. By doing this, he's hoping you'll run back to him and apologize. He expects you to beg him for forgiveness. This is the aggressive approach, where he tries to strong-arm you into submission. He will blame you for everything that went wrong and will guilt trip you, saying how *you* ruined the relationship and making you look like the bad one.

Essentially, he will say anything that provokes and upsets you. And he knows *exactly* what to say to upset you! **Do not give in to his bait and fight back. You will want to defend yourself, but we both know it won't do any good.**

> **Resist the urge—don't say anything!**

He may even call your friends and family to talk to them about it or announce your "sin" on social media. Don't feel a need to explain or justify yourself. If anyone asks, say you left a bad relationship or things didn't work out. And leave it at that.

You're not going to apologize or ask for forgiveness. You are too strong for this and know better now. You escaped and earned your freedom. That's what counts right now.

So focus on this win—*not on winning an impossible argument with him.*

Step 2: Acting nice like he has changed. When the bullying tactics don't work, he will suddenly switch up his approach. He will take some of the blame and say he realized he acted too harshly and needs to be a better partner. He will act super nice, promising to change. At this point, he may already seem changed! If you're religious, he will send you articles and Bible verses that he knows will impact you. In fact, he'll talk about your religion so much, you'll think he's about to convert.

He will use anything he knows is important to you to tug at your heartstrings.

It's tempting to give in because you may feel like he's finally hearing you.

You *want* to believe it. *He is pulling out all the stops and saying everything you've always wanted to hear from him. But these are just empty words.* You need to question if he'll actually follow through on any of the stuff he says or if he actually believes it himself.

Step 3: Finding a replacement for you. In the meantime, he is figuring out an alternative. This alternative likely involves a replacement for you if you don't come back. (Or even if you do come back!) Whatever he gets first—you or the replacement—he will take. He just needs someone to fill the void. You can compare this to a rebound situation, but he's doing it while still trying to get back with you!

Yes, this is hard to hear. But while professing his love to you, he's likely working on grooming someone else. Actually, he may have been doing so for a long time. When he moved you in, he made you his primary supply. This means that while he treats you badly, he still flirts with and treats other women well. As soon as you leave, he'll replace your role with another trapped woman. He'll go from treating her well to treating her badly, like he did to you.

If you are legally married, he may hold off on this or tread more carefully. After all, he will not want to lose his assets in a divorce! But he may still cheat on you without moving the woman in. He will just try harder to retain you as the primary supply and continue to cheat on the side.

> <u>Note:</u> Please don't run back to him now because you're afraid he'll be with another woman. You may feel pain or relief when you hear about it. But remember, you want to be done with him. And if he's spending time with her, that's less time he's spending bothering you. She is sacrificing herself for you, even though she doesn't realize this yet.

He may not succeed in getting a decent replacement. *If he doesn't get one, don't assume that he didn't try!* <u>In this case, he'll try even harder to get you back once he realizes that no one else wants him.</u>

If you go back: If you go back and set new boundaries, he will seem to agree at first. He will say anything to keep you there and be on his best behavior in the beginning. All will seem great for a while. But it's not.

Things are about to get ugly for you! He will punish you for leaving. He will do everything you hate or fear him doing and more. And now he will double down and be much more cautious, so your plans to leave again will be much harder the next time you try.

Story time:

While living in New York with Michael, a neighbor introduced me to Kabbalah, an ancient spiritual wisdom that teaches how we can improve our lives. She said it completely changed her life. Soon, I started taking classes at the Kabbalah Center too. It taught me practical steps to live a much calmer, less reactive life—especially with Michael.

Whenever he started yelling or throwing things, I didn't go into panic mode any more. I pressed pause and just observed instead. I learned to forgo my usual momentary reactions and waited to respond calmly hours or even days later. I stopped feeding the fire with gasoline. Much later, I realized he hated my new behavior. He loved getting emotional reactions out of me and pushed harder when I started behaving like a zen master!

At the time, I thought Kabbalah could help him with his life and improve our relationship. But he kept trash-talking Kabbalah, calling the Center a stupid, corrupt cult. He refused to listen to the positive aspects that changed my life and only criticized it.

After he kicked me out and I didn't crawl back, he changed his tune. His initial aggressive tactics to get me to apologize and come back didn't work. So the next time, he said exactly what I wanted to hear. He admitted that he'd been awful to me and drove me away. For the first time ever, he said he needed to change.

He claimed he picked up my Kabbalah books and notes and started reading them and that he wanted to learn more of their teachings. He even asked if I could email him the class recordings.

Soon he started quoting the teachings, saying they made perfect logical sense to him. He acted like these were huge revelations to him, whereas he'd shamed them just a few weeks before.

At first, I felt relieved and proud that I'd gotten through to him. It seemed too good to be true. But then I asked, "Does he really suddenly believe all this? Or is he just temporarily adopting my beliefs to lure me back in? After I move back in and he gets what he wants, will he just go back to his old ways?" I did not go back.

Within a few months, he moved his new girlfriend in. I think he knew her from his job and worked with her for months or years while we still lived together. Once he had Tessa on his hook, he didn't need me or Kabbalah anymore. I never heard anything about Kabbalah from him again.

> **When he wants something from you, he will say *anything* to get you back—true or not. But once he has what he wants, all that sweet talk and "change" will go right out the window!**

Be ready for any backlash if you don't go back. This might include badmouthing you to everyone who will listen or telling people how great you are and how much he misses you. This is so people give him sympathy and you look bad. They won't suspect the dysfunctional relationship that happened behind closed doors!

Remember: There's a reason why he kept you around for so long, even if he insulted you and called you "difficult" or "annoying." He said that to keep you down so you would feel too bad to leave and would feel lucky to have him. He didn't want you to realize you are way too good for him. But he underestimated your ability to figure him out. Mistreating you wasn't a good long-term strategy for him. It worked at first. But he finally lost you.

Believe it or not, some women never leave because they are so mentally and emotionally beaten down. <u>They believe his lies because he's said the same thing so many times, it becomes an unquestioned truth.</u> The path of least resistance is to stay—and suffer in silence. But you are not that person. **You are strong!**

Staying the course

He may never give up.

Even if many years pass, he may still try to contact you, especially if he's a narcissist. It's been years since I left Vince, and he still tries to contact me once in a while. He reaches out predictably on birthdays and nearly every holiday, through my phone, email, and even social media accounts. I may respond 1 out of every 40 times, but the poor bastard still tries.

These will look like lower-effort attempts than the initial bait. <u>Special occasions are the ultimate excuse.</u> He may start casual and innocent, as if nothing happened and he misses you. His line may be a simple "Happy birthday" or "What are you doing?" or "I miss all the great times we had together."

On the rare times I answer, I never reveal anything important about myself. I tell Vince I'll think about visiting him in New York sometime and wish him well. *I can only respond this way and truly wish him well because it's been years, and he holds no power over me anymore.* I blocked his number for six months after leaving. But now there is no danger I'd ever go back.

<u>If you don't feel strong enough yet to resist his contact attempts, block his number and emails. Change your number if you must.</u>

Do whatever it takes to not get pulled back in!

What if he does really change in the future?

I wouldn't bet on this. But let's just say that there's a small possibility that he saw the error of his ways. What will things look like this time? And how will he treat *you*?

The trouble with established relationship patterns: The problem is the two of you have an established relationship pattern. So even if he has changed, the likelihood that your relationship with him will change is very slim. Think of your childhood friends that you go years without seeing then when you do see them, it almost feels like no time passed. You continue with the same dynamic you've always had, regardless of the fact that you've both likely changed and don't act that way around new adults you befriend. <u>This is because it's hard to change our behavior once we've established relationship dynamics with them. We're prone to settle back into our old, comfortable habits.</u>

Story time:

I've become a lot more outgoing over the years, whereas I previously played the part of a shy, listener type. My childhood best friend, Hannah, used to do all the talking as kids. Whenever I get back together with her, she starts doing the same thing again. Speaking the entire time, as if all I still want to do is listen.

Hannah remembers our old communication dynamics. Despite all my life experiences and changes in personality, it's hard for her to acknowledge my changes and take turns listening. It's also hard for me to break out of my old pattern of listening to her talk constantly.

If I met Hannah for the first time today, I guarantee we wouldn't have this speaking dynamic. We would speak on a more equal basis, like I do with friends from adulthood. Or we wouldn't become friends.

It is nearly impossible to break the dynamics of a longstanding friendship. The same holds true for romantic relationships. You fall back into old patterns.

> *Even if you try to reject his behavior, he thinks he knows you and will try to stretch back to your old boundaries!*

Additionally, first impressions die hard. It's very hard to get someone to change their initial perception of you and accept your new boundaries. They will resist!

Once someone's pigeon-holed you, it takes a lot of work to crawl out of the box they put you in. <u>Humans feel more comfortable putting people into categories. And we are lazy, so we don't want to change anything that seems to already work.</u> So good luck crawling out.

Then there is the whole problem of your personal chemistry. People treat each person differently. Have you ever heard differing opinions about someone? Different people may say completely opposite things about a person's reputation. Someone says someone is the nicest person, but others say he is aggressive. Someone may say a person is honest, but someone else thinks they are untrustworthy.

Why do different people have such varying impressions of the same person? It's because they treat people differently depending on:

• their individual chemistry

• mutual understanding of each other

• past experiences

• the benefits they may get

• any trauma responses they may trigger

• **and most importantly—what they think they can get away with**

Old lovers and old habits. Think of drug addicts. When people get clean, they want to stay away from other people they used to drink or do drugs with. Due to their past history, it's too easy for them to start doing drugs together again. Even if they both eventually change, relapse is still a big risk.

> **It's much easier to start over with someone new so there's no chance of reestablishing these unhealthy patterns.**

So what do you think happens when past partners get back together? There are so many reasons to get into the same patterns again, even if things seem to start well.

If you give him another chance

If you decide to give him another chance, whatever you do, don't move back in yet!

Proceed with caution!

A toxic person spends a lot of time searching for the right target to deploy his tactics on. Once he tags you as someone who is susceptible to his games, he doesn't want to let you go. Like a puppeteer, he knows how to pull the strings to make you turn left or right. <u>Even when you fight back and think you are punishing him, he loves it.</u> After living under his thumb for so long, he likely won't give up without a fight.

You can never win—until you leave.

Are you ready for more of the same?

As soon as you start showing him your boundaries, he might think it's cute at first. He will play along and may agree to your new rules. After all, he will do and say anything at this point to get you back.

But do you think this person is capable and wants to change long term? Do their actions line up with their promises?

If he is a narcissist, the answer is a definite **hell no**. If a narcissist or toxic parent raised him, he may just be carrying out learned programming. If he admits his parents' faults and these unhealthy habits, the answer is **maybe**— with a lot of conscious effort and therapy.

I almost didn't include this section. But I felt the need to distinguish between situations having a high chance and a low chance. In both examples below, the guys are codependents in their thirties, raised by a narcissist father. They both learned and carried out toxic relationship patterns. Please notice the difference:

Story time:

Mark recently escaped a relationship with a narcissist, where his self-esteem was ripped to shreds. Shortly after, he befriended a new coworker, Desiree. They got along perfectly and started dating. Within a year, they moved in together.

He loved her a lot. However, their toxic boss started treating him badly, so he became very high strung. Mark started drinking several energy drinks a day and working harder and longer days. Desiree recognized the bad work environment and found a similar job at another company, as did many of their coworkers. But he stayed at the company, still striving for his boss' approval.

With all the stress from his job, he got triggered by his childhood trauma. So he started raising his voice at Desiree and criticizing her for stupid things that scared her.

Soon after, his girlfriend found another place to live. She ended the relationship and moved out that week. He didn't realize how much his job stress strained his relationship with Desiree.

While he always recognized his father is a narcissist, he is now also very aware of how his learned patterns, shortcomings, and negative behaviors ruined his relationship.

Desiree said she did not want to talk to him for a while, but may want to be friends again someday. Mark is honoring her boundaries and giving her the space she needs.

This is rare to recognize and want to fix the unhealthy patterns. Most people who grew up like this are so steeped in unhealthy patterns, this is normal for them. They don't realize what happened in their childhood was abuse and abnormal and will never see it.

So this is an exceptional case. When the time comes, they could be successful if she's willing to give him another chance. But they would need to start fresh, dating a long time before living together. She would need to pay close attention to ensure he's actually implementing his changes and wasn't all talk. They would need to attend counseling together if negative patterns arose again.

Story time:

Charles had several long-term relationships in the past. All his relationships devolved into verbal abuse and toxic negativity. Then he met Wendy during military training.

When she got injured and lost her job, she moved back home with her parents while she healed. They stayed in the relationship long distance and drove to see each other on weekends. But her parents retired and planned to move overseas. Charles wanted her to marry him and move in with him. She felt rushed, but did it because her parents were moving and she didn't have her own money.

Charles worked in a competitive training environment and became a target. He started blaming Wendy. He said this to her face, his family, and even his bosses. After he came home and unloaded all his anger on her, he would tell her that she was the one making him miserable. He even talked about her leaving, suggesting he'd be better off without her.

Wendy took him seriously and moved out to her aunt's house. She felt sad but actually believed that he might do better at work without her around.

Charles ignored her at first, then started lashing out and provoking her. She fought back.

Within a few weeks, he saw his strategy wasn't working because she didn't come running back. So he changed his tune. He said he didn't actually want a divorce. He gave positive feedback on relationship articles she'd sent him about being a good husband and said he's working on it. He mailed her his Bible with a bunch of sticky notes and highlighted verses. Wendy still loves him and wants to believe he will change.

But he never admitted any wrongdoing. And previously, he refused to keep going to marriage counseling after the counselor sided with Wendy once. Charles also won't acknowledge that anything is wrong with his family, even though his father and sister are narcissists who pick on him and badmouth Wendy. Yet he often criticizes Wendy's family for their unhealthy behaviors.

If someone doesn't see anything wrong with the unhealthy dynamics they grew up in, how can they change them?

Do you see any red flags with Charles and Wendy? He does not realize that his family is toxic and he adopted their patterns, but is quick to point out all of Wendy and her family's faults. Wendy readily admits her family is screwed up.

Charles' unwillingness to even see his faults are a deal breaker. Yet, Wendy's financial dependence on him is clouding her judgment. As soon as she moves back, she loses any upper hand and will be subject to his behavior. She needs to find a decent-paying job and her own place, and see if he will admit his negative patterns in therapy, before she considers moving back in.

> **No matter the situation, becoming financially independent and confident, having your own place, and living your own life levels the playing field so you can truly decide whether someone is a good partner for you, not whether you need them financially or if it's more convenient for you to stay there.**

Were you ever on a level playing field while dating him? Or was staying always a matter of financial stability, survival, or the feeling of having a family to go home to?

Are both of you willing to admit what you did wrong in the relationship and put in the effort to improve yourselves? <u>If one doesn't, it won't work.</u> If both can admit faults and put in the effort, there is a chance of success.

～❧

If he sort of wants you back (sexually)

If he's not a narcissist or similar, it will still be natural for him to miss you. He may even feel bad about what happened. He might keep in contact with you, but might not be as pushy as a more toxic partner. *In his heart, he probably knows you are not good for each other too.*

If you do stay in contact with him, keep him at arm's length, and his motive will become clear over time.

Sex and attention

He may not be ready to lose your attention and company. It's easy to get pulled back into something known and comfortable when you're both lonely. He may even need sex and hasn't been able to score since the breakup. Many male friends have told me they will try to hit up previous sexual partners when they get horny and desperate, because they're easier targets. They admit it's a lazy way of getting women.

As a female, it is harder for us to separate love and the physical act of sex. The oxytocin hormone released during sex makes us feel bonded and connected to our partner. Yes, it feels good in the moment but does this benefit your well-being?

Keep your distance with this one. If he starts talking romantically to you again, tell him you're not ready to go there. Don't jump right back on the cowboy once you've gone through all this trouble to leave.

❧

If he seems glad you're gone

If he doesn't try hard to get you back, you are lucky.

It could mean he either:

• isn't super toxic,

• saw it was a bad relationship,

• knows he lost you and is focused on another unassuming target,

• is waiting for the right moment to strike,

• or wanted you gone and thought it was his idea.

However, don't fully let your guard down yet. It's better to be safe than sorry. *You still don't want to tell him where you live and still should change your daily routines, just in case.*

It's also best to limit your communication and time spent around him. It may be possible to become friends in the *far future*, but right now isn't a good time to stay in close contact with each other.

Don't feel sad about this or assume he never loved you or doesn't miss you. Just because he doesn't say it, doesn't mean it's not true. Be thankful that he isn't as bad as you thought. <u>Both of you can use this time to heal from each other.</u>

The truth about the other woman

The likelihood is high that he'll look for another woman. Do you feel jealous at all? Do you think he'll ultimately treat her any better than he treated you?

Don't go back because you're sad or jealous he'll find someone else. You should actually be *thankful* when he does.

Story time:

At first, I felt sad and upset when Michael told me about Tessa. He'd just been coaxing me to move back in, then suddenly he's serious with someone else. He moved her in a few months after I left. When I went to gather my things, I saw paintings from art classes he had taken Tessa to. I had begged him to go to fun adult art classes with me, and he'd refused. Then he had told me he was not interested in sex anymore, so I felt enraged when he told me he was having sex with her. I felt sad when I saw them walking down the street, happily chatting, instead of him scowling.

I cried to my close friend, saying that I can't believe how much better he treats her than he did me. My friend reminded me that he treated me great in the beginning too. And soon he will treat Tessa the same way he treated me.

At this point, we didn't even know what a narcissist was or that Michael was one of them. But we now know a narcissist follows this typical pattern. They love bomb you and show you a fun time in the beginning. Then once they trap you into marriage, kids, or living together, they take it all away. That's when their true, boring, and abusive selves come out. They will do this to *every* partner eventually, even the new one after you.

It took several months of perspective, but I finally felt relieved that he had moved Tessa in. That way he focused his attention on her and stopped bothering me to lure me back. *The realization finally hit me that I finally broke free from him!*

If he's definitely not a narcissist, your circumstances might be different. He might actually treat someone else better than you long term. But so what? Maybe they make a better match.

Your ex wasn't treating *you* well—which is your only concern.

Even if it's possible for him to improve and treat you better, he's shown you that he's not going to do it while he already has you there. He feels too comfortable. It's going to take a big wake-up call to move him to see the problem. He's going to need time alone to figure that out and miss you. Staying or running right back won't solve anything.

If you miss him

It is totally normal to miss him, even at the end of a bad relationship. He was part of your daily life. Humans are creatures of habit and comfort. Even with all the problems, you had some comfort in the routine, predictability, and knowledge he would be there. He always eventually came home, even if things weren't good. And now that is gone. So it is normal to miss him.

Story time:

A college friend named Rae told me how she realized her fiancé was the one. They fought all the time, but when he moved out for a few months, she missed him so much. It felt unbearable to go on without him. She said that's how she knew.

He moved back in and proposed. A few years later, she popped up on social media. She and the guy married and had a kid together, but they divorced soon after. Guess missing him all the time didn't mean he was the right guy!

Maybe you see your friends on Facebook who post tons of pictures of them looking happy with their sweetie. Then one day the pics are suddenly deleted, and they changed their last name back to their maiden name. Learn from their mistakes!

Good sexual chemistry and strong feelings mean you were on the same frequency and self-esteem level at that point in time. It says nothing about long-term relationship longevity, or whether the person is good for you.

How intensely you miss someone is not an indicator that they are the one. <u>If anything, you will miss a toxic partner more than a healthy partner.</u> Because it's not them you miss—it's all the cycles of ups and downs they created. During your time with him, you became obsessed with how he thinks and feels. He became your hobby. This happened unintentionally. You simply wanted to understand him to improve your relationship. So you went above and beyond and tried everything to make it work.

<u>And now your brain is addicted to the drama and excitement and is going through withdrawals.</u> So, yes, it will take some time to adjust to your new normal.

> **With plenty of distractions and a healthy new normal, your brain will become rewired.**

This is similar to a drug addict getting off drugs. It's very painful at first. But the reward of being clean is too great to pass up. You'll feel so relieved you left and stayed out in the end.

Some strategies can help keep you occupied so you are way less likely to go back. The way to solve missing the drama or the ups and downs is to replace this stimulus with another stimulus! Only this time, choose something positive.

<u>**Strategies to replace the missing drama**</u>

If you

- had a lot of ups and downs in your relationship or
- spent a large amount of time worrying or thinking about what he's going to do next, or
- worried about what you should do next,

you are just missing the drama. <u>So now you need to manage your withdrawals.</u>

It's super difficult to break out of mental patterns that you've been practicing for months, or maybe years. So don't beat yourself up for still thinking about him all the time. This is natural!

But to combat this, you need to replace the drama with new interests.

> **If you want to permanently get rid of an old habit, your best bet is to replace it with a new habit.**

So you want to replace obsessing about his moods and reactions to something else. It's best if the new habit is <u>similar in intensity.</u>

<u>Note:</u> This isn't optional. If you don't replace this new space with a new interest, the old one will eat you alive.

The good news is, you are getting a new lease on life. Not only will you have your own place, where you won't have to worry about constant drama, but you also no longer need to expend energy on him. *This frees up a huge chunk of mind space to pursue new interests!*

It's time for you to brainstorm some ideas.

What is something exciting you've always wanted to do, but never got into? Something you didn't have the time for, or that he didn't approve of?

Athletics, training, and competition: Athletic endeavors, such as running, bicycling, tennis, wall climbing, and playing on a soccer team are some great options. These require mental and physical coordination and lots of time spent practicing. Bonus points if you practice this sport outdoors. Spending time in the sun and outdoors makes us feel happier due to the production of vitamin D and serotonin, and gives us a stronger feeling of well-being.

Train for a marathon or race if you feel up to it. This will take discipline and commitment, which gives you a goal and can help raise your confidence levels.

Swimming and yoga are sports that everyone can do—so no excuses! Swimming is great because it's low impact, for those who have joint or weight issues or simply don't like to run. Yoga can be as easy or challenging as you make it. Just start at the beginner's level and find your comfort level from there.

Physical training helps manage stress, moodiness, anxiety, and pain, which are often side effects of toxic relationships. <u>Physical activity floods your body with positive hormones like endorphins and serotonin.</u> These hormones make you feel happier and boost your mood. Exercise improves your mind and body, too. So you can be proud of yourself for this.

> <u>Pro tip:</u> The more rigorously you exercise, the more benefits you'll get. You need to get your heart rate up and challenge yourself. So many people underestimate this small lifestyle

adjustment. Try to incorporate this into your life before going on any medications for anxiety or depression. Exercise may be all you need. If you feel intimidated, start small by taking a brisk 15-minute walk in your neighborhood each day.

Learning a fun skill: You can learn a new skill, such as chess, a musical instrument, or singing. It works best if it's something physical or requires lots of mental concentration. You need to occupy the huge void in your mind so you don't leave time to ruminate. If you fill this space in your life, you're less likely to miss him or the drama. This reduces your risk of going back to him out of boredom, habit, and comfort.

You don't want to go too wild with something that's super difficult or expensive. Beware of jumping into a graduate school program or another huge commitment. *This is a time to have fun and explore.*

Ask your friends: If you're having trouble thinking of a new hobby, you can ask friends about their hobbies. Most would be glad to bring you with them and introduce you to their hobby.

You need to spend time around other people. Not just anyone—it's ideal if they are positive people you already trust. Those who remember your amazing personality and traits. They can help lift you out of the rut you're in and get you back to normalcy.

Your entire life will begin to improve

Look, you may miss him, so it will really suck—at first. But it will get better.

No, your life won't become better overnight. If you lived with him for a long time, it will get harder before it gets better. You will wonder and worry if and when he'll contact you next. You'll think about whether you'll run into him at the grocery store. Nightmares of him finding you or mistreating you might come up. You may get angry and want to lash out at him for ruining the relationship or treating you like crap. Maybe you feel shame about your relationship ending and worry about how you'll explain yourself to others.

This is all normal. *If you didn't feel all this loss and pain, you wouldn't be human.*

But just know that each small gain will add up. Maybe you might not like the place you moved into because it's not as nice as the one before. Or you'll worry if you can actually hold down your own job to make enough money to pay all your bills yourself. <u>Don't worry, this self-sufficiency thing feels new now, but it's like re-learning to walk again after not using your legs for months or years.</u> It will feel strange and unfamiliar at first, but you'll keep getting stronger and better. One day, you'll forget you ever forgot how to walk.

This could look like you getting a raise or a better-paying job more suited to your talents. And now you can watch your bank account grow and make new, positive friends who will cheer you on. It doesn't happen right away, but it gets better over time.

> **It may take several months to notice improvements and you will probably be doing great long before you notice it.**

But other people will tell you how much you smile and that you seem happier. You may notice any previous health issues aren't bothering you so much, and you don't need to take as many medications or supplements as you used to. <u>You'll look forward to going home to peace and quiet instead of bracing yourself for what might be waiting for you.</u>

All this triples if you stop talking to him! The less contact you have with him or other toxic people, the less anxiety you'll have.

> **The more positive thoughts and people you have in your life, the faster you will heal.**

The tension you've been holding onto will dissipate. For me, I held a lot of tension in my face. Other people told me my face looked different a few months after moving in with Vince. For many months after leaving, I massaged my face every day. I did this almost every single time after washing my hands. One day, my facial muscles stopped feeling tight. Around that time, people told me that I looked different and my face actually looked prettier!

Once you're not feeling as defensive, anxious, or fearful, you let go of a lot. *Your energy changes, and people notice!* You start making eye contact with people more and feel more open to making friendships with others.

> **And since your happiness affects others' moods, too, you feel more confident and other people want to be around you.**

The day will come where you can look back and laugh at the situation you were in. It will seem crazy that you were too afraid to move out and look for your own place. It won't make sense that you hesitated to apply for jobs you are totally qualified for. Or that you considered a man to be your family and partner, when he did not treat you the way you deserve.

You'll wonder why you felt so trapped when the door was open the entire time. It was all an illusion! Our minds can't think straight when someone we trust is purposely confusing us.

～⬌

Chapter 7 review

Go no contact if possible

• If you have no reason to speak to him, don't.

• Block his number or don't reply to his messages.

The grey rock method alternative

• If you have legal ties, like kids with him or other legal obligations, and must communicate—use the grey rock method.

• Communicate with him only about issues that pertain to joint property or interests.

• Keep it brief, emotionless, and on topic.

• Don't let him guilt trip you about the relationship or push your buttons.

• If he acts up, save his messages and report them to your lawyer.

If he tries to suck you back in

• If you didn't leave on his terms, he will likely try to contact you.

• He may chastise, bully, and guilt trip you. If this doesn't work, he'll apologize and promise to change. He will pull out all the stops to get you back into his lair.

• He may be talking to other women as a backup plan already, despite his sweet words toward you. *Don't let his sweet words of undying love, caring, and changing fool you.*

• If you give in and go back, he'll eventually punish you for leaving. Things won't improve, and you'll be in a worse place than when you started.

• If he's not a narcissist, he may learn a lesson from this relationship and change. But once someone pigeonholes you and establishes the relationship dynamics, it's hard to change that pattern.

• Things may start well, but it's easy to devolve into old habits. Change is hard and rare. With you living in his lair, his life is convenient and comfortable. He wants it to be that way again.

• If you move out, he might improve. But as soon as you give up your upper hand of living separately, it's too easy for him to go back to his old ways.

• If you give him another chance, whatever you do, don't move back in!

• *Don't go back to him for financial reasons or a place to stay.* Level the playing field by choosing him for how he treats you, not what he can offer you or what you materially need from him.

If he sort of wants you back (sexually)

• It's natural for him to miss your attention and company, especially the sex you had.

• It isn't a good idea to hook up and will only emotionally confuse you and prolong your suffering.

If he seems glad you're gone

• Consider yourself lucky.

• Don't let your guard down yet. Limit contact with him and don't reveal details about yourself, such as your schedule or where you live.

• In the far future, you may become friends. But use this space apart to heal.

• If he finds another woman and treats her better than you, *only focus on how he treated you.* He wasn't willing to treat you better while you lived together.

If you miss him

• This is normal and painful at first. But do you miss *him* or do you miss the emotional ups and downs? Or someone being there?

• *How intensely you miss someone is not an indicator that you belong together.*

• To get rid of an old habit, replace it with a new habit! Do this with friends for companionship or so they can teach you their hobbies.

• Physical endurance training is a great choice because it also releases feel-good hormones like endorphins and serotonin. They help you naturally handle pain, stress, and moodiness.

<u>Your entire life will begin to improve</u>

• Big life changes are hard. You will likely feel worse before you feel better.

• Slowly but surely, things will get better. This could take several weeks or several months, but then one day, you'll realize how much better you feel.

• Your energy will change, and you'll start attracting better people and situations into your life.

Conclusion

C ONGRATULATIONS FOR FINISHING THIS book and leaving
your toxic partner! I hope this book helped you navigate how to leave
a toxic partner safely and not return. I have given you a lot of steps and
considerations. I hope you easily found and applied the respective advice to
your situation.

Don't feel foolish for having been in this situation. You fell in love and got
burned. He knew your weak points and saw an opening. He traded material
benefits and "family" support for your personality and company. He got you
addicted to seeking his approval using the intermittent reinforcement tactic.
Using tools and tricks is the only way he can get women to stick around,
which is why he perfected this luring technique.

But the good news is, once you leave him, you will be safe. You will be so
much stronger for experiencing this and bravely leaving, even if it doesn't feel
that way now.

Now you realize your mistake and how you got stuck, and it won't happen
again. You will keep your upper hand in the future, even if you live with
someone else. You will always retain some independence and earn your own
income. *No man will ever put you in a position where you feel trapped by your
financial situation.*

Good luck in the future and keep growing stronger. I know you can do it, because I did it! Live life on your own terms, and you can do anything you set your mind to! Don't ever allow the limits someone else placed on you to stop you. Now you are free to push the reset button and pursue your own dreams this time.

Can You Help?

Thank You For Reading My Book!

I really appreciate all of your feedback, and I love hearing what you have to say.

I need your input to make the next version of this book and my future books better.

Please leave me an honest review on Amazon letting me know what you thought of the book.

Please rate my book on Amazon and Goodreads

Thanks so much!

Christy

About the Author

Christy Piper is a human dynamics, mindset, and relationship expert. She learned these lessons the hard way when she was forced to handle dysfunctional personal and professional relationships. She developed strategies to rise above her circumstances. Now she helps others uncover their own strength and resilience. She is the wise older sister and cool professor you always wanted. Christy received her undergraduate and graduate degrees from Florida State University and is a US Navy veteran. She currently lives in New England.

Follow me on **Amazon** and **Goodreads** for updates on my future work. You can also find me on **www.christypiper.com.**

Coming soon to all formats, including hardcover and audiobook

Visit http://www.christypiper.com/gydm-bonus/ to receive your Freedom Checklist bonus.